C000179617

The World's Greatest Shooting Stories is a collection of remarkable true-life tales from across the world. Focusing on the past two hundred years of sporting shooting it includes stories of big game hunting in Africa and India in the nineteenth century, Edwardian pheasant and grouse shooting and sport in the modern world.

The World's Greatest Shooting Stories also includes wildfowling tales and stories of poachers, inexplicable incidents, ghostly happenings and one in a million shots.

Here you will discover everything from delightfully dotty Royals – like George V, who always went shooting with a loader deliberately chosen because he looked exactly like the king – to elderly generals who took their trousers off before going elephant shooting, Russian secret service sportsmen who took pot shots at the beaters and American diplomats who went wildfowling by helicopter.

The great shooting characters of the past are well-represented – men like Sir Ralph Payne-Gallwey and Colonel Peter Hawker who devoted their lives to sporting shooting – but dozens of other, less well known sportsmen are also included.

Here, among numerous delightful characters, you will find John Mytton, a Shropshire squire who insisted on wildfowling in the depths of winter in his nightshirt, together with a Mr Toomey who taught his pet pig to point and retrieve, and Lord Malmesbury who, in forty seasons, calculated that he had walked 36,200 miles or very nearly one and a half times round the world in pursuit of a total bag of 38,934. To achieve that bag he had fired 54,987 shots!

Tom Quinn has written many books about the history of the English countryside as well as books on shooting, and fishing. He has edited a number of magazines including *The Countryman* and is editor of *Country Landowner*.

THE WORLD'S GREATEST SHOOTING STORIES

THE WORLD'S GREATEST SHOOTING STORIES

TOM QUINN

Quiller

Copyright © 2010 Tom Quinn

First published in the UK in 2010
by Quiller, an imprint of Quiller Publishing Ltd

British Library Cataloguing-in-Publication Data
A catalogue record for this book
is available from the British Library

ISBN 978 1 84689 084 0

The right of Tom Quinn to be identified as the author of this work has been asserted in accordance with the Copyright, Design and Patent Act 1988

The information in this book is true and complete to the best of our knowledge. All recommendations are made without any guarantee on the part of the Publisher, who also disclaims any liability incurred in connection with the use of this data or specific details.

All rights reserved. No part of this book may be reproduced or transmitted in any form or by any means, electronic or mechanical including photocopying, recording or by any information storage and retrieval system, without permission from the Publisher in writing.

Printed in the UK by MPG Books Group

Quiller

An imprint of Quiller Publishing Ltd
Wykey House, Wykey, Shrewsbury, SY4 1JA
Tel: 01939 261616 Fax: 01939 261606
E-mail: info@quillerbooks.com
Website: www.countrybooksdirect.com

Contents

Introduction

Shooting for sport and for the pot has a long and eventful history. In the earliest days, when putting something on the table was the prime concern, there was little idea of giving quarry species a sporting chance – birds were shot at roost or well before they could get airborne. If there was a chance that one shot would bag a dozen birds the sportsman always took it.

But as shotguns developed, and particularly with the invention of the breechloader, the idea developed that there was little point shooting at an easy target – a sitting duck as it were – and that far more enjoyment could be had by pursuing difficult, high-flying birds. Better to shoot one good bird than a dozen birds that offered no challenge.

With the birth of the sport of shooting flying, as it was known early on, came stories of extraordinary shots, bizarre events, ghostly incidents, remarkable coincidences.

And as the British Empire expanded in the nineteenth century, tales of extraordinary sport from across the world began to filter back to England. In the days when shooting warranted regular coverage in the national newspapers, these stories attracted huge reader interest. Many of the sportsmen involved became, in a small way, heroes who took huge risks in remote places to bag what were seen then as extremely dangerous animals.

Of course in the nineteenth century there was little idea of conservation and it was simply assumed that the world was such a big place that no amount of shooting could ever put a particular species at risk of extinction. We know better now, of course, but the stories from that distant world still make wonderful reading and it is the best, and most extraordinary of these tales that are gathered here. Most have been collected from long-forgotten books, magazines and newspapers; many concern men whose exploits often formed the basis of books that were, in their time, best sellers. But what they all have in common is a sense of adventure; a sense that the challenges of a world only then opening up for the first time might provide something truly worth writing home about.

A note on the text

The stories in this book have been collected over many years from a wide variety of sources, but mostly from out of print books, magazines and journals. I've also spent long, enjoyable hours poring over rare books in The British Library. Chance played its part, too. A copy of *The Newcastle Chronicle* discovered in an old drawer and dating from the first half of the nineteenth century yielded one story. Another came from an ancient, bedraggled charity shop book that had lost its cover and title page. One or two tales I heard from elderly friends and colleagues.

It always amuses me to think that a number of the best stories in the book came from Philip Brown, who, despite successfully editing *The Shooting Times* magazine for a number of years, never actually shot at all.

1 Muzzleloaders and Mavericks

Gunning for the minister

The Scottish minister was a keen shooting man who got on very well with the local keeper, but the churchman had noticed that, for some months past, the keeper had ceased to come to church. This was in the 1950s when, in small communities, everyone knew precisely what everyone else was up to. The minister decided it was his duty to do something about this terrible lapse. He met the keeper at the end of a shooting day and asked what was going on.

'Well,' said the keeper, 'I don't come to church because I don't want to upset you or the church services.'

'I don't understand?' said the minister.

'Well, it's like this,' said the keeper. 'If I go to church on a Sunday the whole parish will know it and they'll all go poaching since I'm the only man who can stop them. If I stay away from church none of the men of the village will dare to go poaching so they might as well go to church, which they do. So if I turn up to church you'll be preaching to empty pews and I wouldn't want that on my conscience!'

With that the keeper broke away and carried on loading the game cart. The minister, sensible enough to know when he'd been out manoeuvred, beat a hasty retreat.

Goose shooting by aeroplane

One of the greatest wildfowlers of all time, Stanley Duncan, shot geese and duck all along the Wash and the Norfolk coast and elsewhere. His pursuit of sport verged on the fanatical – if one man could be said to have devoted his life to wildfowling it was certainly Duncan. A lifetime of shooting produced many startling days and none more so than when he helped a pilot friend use an aeroplane for goose shooting.

Duncan carried out his reconnaissance with care. A field close to the windswept coast of Yorkshire where the geese were known to feed regularly was left undisturbed for several weeks but the birds were watched closely.

When enough birds felt safe on the field the plan began to unfold. The idea was that the pilot would take off and then fly low over the hedge at the edge of the field where the geese were feeding. This was supposed to put the birds up, but it would also drive them forward toward two Guns waiting at the other end the field.

The first attempt was a flop. The plane came over the hedge but long before it arrived the geese, hearing a most ungodly noise, took off vertically before swinging quickly away to the left well out of range of the Guns.

The pilot landed a few miles away and the Gunners waited. A few hours later a big party of geese arrived and began to feed. By this time the wind was howling, which may explain why, on the second attempt, the birds did not hear the plane's engine until it cleared the hedge with a roar that so astonished the birds that rather than take off they simply lay doggo. A shot from one of the Guns reminded them that their best bet was to get out of the field as fast as possible – with a mighty clatter of wings they wheeled away downwind, but the presence of the plane kept them low to the ground. Some landed in a hedge bottom, others managed to gain height before the plane, turning quickly, got above the flock again and pushed it towards the Guns who scored several rights and lefts.

Elaborate and expensive the experiment, though counted a success, was never tried again.

Tree tops

There are many instances where shooting men become so devoted to the pursuit of a particular species that they pretty much lose interest in everything else. The great pigeon shooter Archie Coats is a good example – he spent much of the latter part of his life in various hides in fields across Hampshire waiting for the grey birds to come in.

But a Victorian shot might have outdone even the great Archie Coats in his enthusiasm for pigeons. Unlike Archie, who decoyed his birds onto fields of wheat or rapeseed, our Victorian Gun – whose antics were reported in a number of long vanished sporting papers – was entirely devoted to roost shooting. He loved nothing more than to stand in a wood at dusk and wait for the birds to come in to the high tree tops. It was great sport and he was so devoted to it that he decided it would be a good idea to 'get up there among 'em' by which he meant he wanted to shoot the birds, not from the base of the trees, but from the level at which the birds came in. To do it he had a special platform built at the edge of the wood. It involved weeks of work to create an elaborate wooden structure – rather like an electricity pylon – which was then covered in foliage to make it blend in with the rest of the trees.

The Gun allowed several weeks for the birds to get used to the new structure and then set off for his first evening shoot. It was far more exciting he decided than shooting from the ground and he was far more successful than usual. But the number of birds he was able to shoot quickly declined until it was hardly worth bothering. He tried resting the wood for weeks, then for a whole summer but when he returned once the leaves had fallen the birds still seemed very reluctant to return to the wood. It was baffling. The shooter gave up and concentrated his attentions on shooting other woods from the ground.

A few years passed and he tried the platform again. It had decayed a little and climbing to the top was a dangerous business. As darkness fell hardly a bird approached the wood. He decided to have the tower demolished. Weeks after it had come crashing down he tried shooting the wood at dusk from the ground and was amazed to see the pigeon coming in the sort of numbers not seen since long before he built his tower.

Wife beater

Mrs David Stanhope had accompanied her husband to Yorkshire for a week's grouse shooting. He was wildly enthusiastic and had high hopes of the coming sport, but his first day in the butts was so bad that he became morose and depressed.

Asleep that night he seemed, deep in his unconscious brain, to re-live his terrible day in the field. He thrashed about in his sleep shouting 'Bird over!' or 'God damn this gun' or 'how the hell did I miss that?'

His terrible dream lasted more than an hour but his wife feared to wake him, believing that it would be better for him to get his first bad day fully out of his system. But the next day he fared little better and grew ever more gloomy. At dinner he hardly spoke and ate nothing.

That second night the shouting and thrashing about were even worse and she decided to wake him. 'Mark over!' he shouted at the top of his voice and then 'Leg down bird!'

Eventually he woke, apologised and promptly fell asleep again. Within minutes the ranting and raving had resumed. On the next night things were even worse – indeed the situation was so bad that he continually lashed out while his terrified wife tried to dodge the blows. Despite her best efforts to avoid his flailing fists, she eventually received a terrific punch in the eye and was forced to either leave the hotel or explain the black eye. She decided on the former option and returned to London on the morning train leaving her husband to wrestle with his demons alone.

Experimental shots

Shooting men have always been famous for their eccentricity, but the Edwardians and Victorians were perhaps the most eccentric sportsmen of all. A wealthy landowner writing to a sporting magazine in the late 1880s described what must be the most eccentric series of scientific experiments in history.

The idea occurred to him that he should test the effectiveness of various forms of clothing at protecting people from shotgun pellets!

On shooting days on his estate he had noticed that his beaters were occasionally hit by stray shot. If the shot simply fell out of the sky (coming down with the aid of gravity following a shot at a high bird) it pattered like rain on the beater's back and head and did little or no harm, but if they were hit at anything between one hundred and two hundred yards and with shot fired directly from a gun, they were left bleeding and in pain.

With this in mind the landowner carried out a series of experiments – in a way that now seems foolhardy to the point of madness – into the relative merits of different types of clothing as 'shot blockers'.

To be fair he at least made himself the subject of his dangerous experiments rather than ask his beaters. He tried wearing tweed, heavy cotton corduroy and a number of other fabrics in varying combinations and then asked a friend to fire different shot sizes at him at distances of 120 to 150 yards.

'It was perfectly safe,' he told his the magazine editor, 'as I told my servant to be sure to fire only at my legs.'

After several days of shooting and several dozen shots he was quite badly hurt with blood streaming down his legs and dozens of nasty wounds. But he was delighted with his experiment and announced that for maximum protection in the field several thick pairs of corduroys were probably best if leather trousers were unavailable.

Double trouble

King George V always wore a beard, which seems today to place him even further back in history than he really was. His beard may also make him look far more serious than he really was. In fact he was something of an eccentric who loved practical jokes.

While shooting at Sandringham, for example, he insisted that one of the estate workers should load for him rather than his own loader. The result was muddled and confused shooting, which seemed not to bother the king at all.

It took the king's friends some time to realise that the reason he liked this particular loader was that the man could have been his twin. The estate worker was the same height and build and – best of all – sported a beard the very image of the king's.

Whether by accident or design the king and his loader began gradually to wear the same clothes. At first it was just that their coats were similar, then their breeks and shoes and stockings. The loader was of a similar build to the king and this combined with the similarity of clothing and of course the beard created a remarkable effect that many commented on at the time. If the king had objected to the obvious similarity he might have done something about it – ordered the loader to shave perhaps – but he was clearly delighted at the whole thing, perhaps because it meant that neither his shooting guests, nor the beaters or household servants was ever quite sure who was addressing whom. The loader seems to have been highly amused by the whole thing too – particularly when he found himself addressed in highly deferential terms by earls, dukes and foreign heads of state.

Trench foot

The great events of the First World War and the slaughter and waste of that conflict are well known, but amid the human carnage animals and birds carried on much as before. Pheasants and partridges flourished all along the western front where soldiers from Britain, France and Germany died in their millions. Many soldiers commented on the fact that game birds seemed if anything to have increased in number –

perhaps because sporting shooting had ended for the duration. When they weren't perched on a broken stump of a tree in the middle of no man's land they could be found grazing gently across the shell-pocked ground and close up against the firing line and soldiers frequently disturbed hares on their forms. Bizarre though the whole thing sounds it actually made sense from the animals' point of view.

During lulls in the fighting one or two soldiers who had been keen on game shooting at home took the chance to supplement their rations by pursuing an occasional bird.

Among the officers, walking stick shotguns were popular and on at least one occasion a group of officers enjoyed a most successful outing on fields just a few hundred yards behind the front line trenches. They bagged several pheasants and then noticed that the Germans had clearly heard the shots and assumed there was a battery in the area for seconds later the air was filled with the sound of screaming shells heading toward them. They beat a hasty retreat.

On another occasion, as he recorded in his memoirs, Lieutenant Galwey Foley described a day in 1916 when he heard pheasants just behind the front line trenches. He decided to have a go for them. Galwey Foley had hunted pheasants and other birds in and around the trenches many times before so he knew the ropes – the trick was to stalk your birds by dashing from shell hole to shell hole. This sounds more dangerous than it perhaps was – hitting a quickly moving target (Lieutenant Galwey Foley) would always be more a matter of luck than judgment using the rifles then in use.

Despite a few falls into old shell holes Galwey quickly got within sight of a small group of pheasants, took careful aim with his rifle and bagged one. He stuffed it inside his coat and beat a hasty retreat to his own trench in time for breakfast.

Partridges were particularly plentiful over the trenches but very difficult to hit with a single bullet from a rifle. In letters home Galwey Foley complained again and again that he was sorely in need of a shotgun for these birds, but it is doubtful if the army would have looked kindly on a request for a 12 bore.

Galwey Foley seems always to have had an eye on the sporting possibilities of life in the trenches. On one occasion he heard the unmistakable sound of geese flighting towards the German lines. He shouted at the men on the British firing step to give the birds rapid fire in the hope of bringing one down. The birds passed unscathed and then, to his astonishment, he noticed that as the birds reached the German trenches they were greeted by a similar fusillade, but with the same result.

Mornings in the trenches for Galwey Foley were devoted to shooting rats with his revolver – the rats, described in a number of memoirs as being as big as cats, had grown fat from eating the huge numbers of dead soldiers left out in no man's land.

History might have been different...

The assassination of Archduke Franz Ferdinand of Austria was the spark that ignited the Great War. However, a little-known incident at an English shooting estate long before 1914 might have ended the Archduke's life and thereby changed the course of history.

The archduke had been a guest of the sixth Duke of Portland, a keen shot who was well connected right across Europe and frequently had foreign heads of state to stay. He tended to mix his shooting parties so in addition to foreign monarchs and princes he invited the best British shots. Thus it was common to find that the guests at a Portland shooting day included the King of Spain, King Carlos of Portugal several English dukes and earls and, of course, Archduke Franz Ferdinand of Austria himself. Franz Ferdinand was by all accounts a fine shot who quickly got used to the high-flying birds on offer at the Portland estate. After observing his guest's shooting for a few days Portland pronounced him 'certainly the equal of most of my friends'.

During a shoot in December 1913 the archduke found he had been allotted a place on a drive where there was deep snow. He began the drive well and built up a good rhythm with his two loaders; then, without warning one of them slipped and fell. The gun the man was carrying went off as it hit the ground and both barrels were discharged, the shot passing within a foot of the archduke's head.

No doubt the Great War would have happened anyway, but one wonders if it might not all have been very different if the archduke had died in England rather than at Sarajevo little more than a year later.

Obsessed by sport

One of the greatest sportsmen of the nineteenth and early twentieth century, Frederick Courtenay Selous spent virtually the whole of his adult life pursuing game in distant corners of the world.

Born in 1851 Selous lived until 1917. He began shooting at the age of six and was, in addition, an avid butterfly collector. His years at Rugby school were largely spent wildfowling, egg collecting and rough shooting – and being beaten for missing lessons. On one occasion he walked fifteen miles and climbed a sixty-foot high tree to obtain a pair of heron eggs. In winter he regularly swam out across half frozen lakes to retrieve duck and geese he'd shot, but his most extraordinary exploits took place in Africa, where, for example, he once shot twenty-two elephants in a day.

One of his most bizarre habits was always to remove his trousers when elephant hunting. He would wait until the elephant was within range before stripping off – no one ever really discovered why he did this but it seemed to work well for him as he rarely missed or bungled his shot. He worried little about the quality of the guns he used – when his London rifle was stolen he simply bought a homemade African 4 bore and used that instead. It was a terrible gun weighing nearly 20 pounds and in constant danger of exploding, but Selous simply didn't care.

In his numerous books on shooting Selous waxes lyrical about the seemingly endless supply of African game but he seems to have eaten little of what he shot. His diet was reputed to consist of moose, deer or antelope fat and very strong tea.

After a lifetime of adventure Selous aged sixty-three still felt compelled to join up when the Great War started in 1914. He was killed in East Africa aged sixty-five while leading his men against a vastly superior force of Germans.

Mad hatter

Lord Walsingham was a brilliant shot and a passionate entomologist. He was an avid collector of birds (many were shot and stuffed to order for the British Museum) butterflies, moths, beetles and other insects. He was a familiar face in the Fens of East Anglia and particularly at Wicken Fen, which is now owned by the National Trust.

Whether shooting or insect hunting Walsingham was invariably dressed in the oddest of fashions – in this respect he was perhaps the most eccentric of all Victorian sportsmen. He wore a huge moleskin jacket that really was made from moleskin, a snakeskin waistcoat and a hat made from a large, whole hedgehog skin with its spines intact. Walsingham deliberately had two large glass eyes fitted to the hat to complete the picture.

The hedgehog's head fitted neatly between Walsingham's eyes rather like the face guard on a Saxon warrior's helmet.

Peasant shooting

A guest at one of Sweden's most famous old estates saw a hare coming towards him but decided not to shoot it as the beaters were already in view and he judged that the shot would not be entirely safe.

'Why didn't you shoot?' asked the Englishman's host.

'I thought the beaters were too close and the shot would have been unsafe,' came the reply

'You must not worry about these things,' said the host, 'in Sweden we have many peasants, but few hares.'

Mercury man

He had made a great deal of money in the booming hat trade of Victorian England. His small shop and factory in Luton, Bedfordshire – then the centre of Britain's hat making industry – had expanded and he was now a very rich man. He invested in land and then more land. His great passion gradually became shooting and he employed several experienced keepers to ensure that his birds were the best in the county.

He bought a pair of London guns – the finest money could buy – and organised two formal shooting days a week right through the season. During his first season his wealthier friends and neighbours were happy to come and shoot with him but his strange behaviour put most of them off and by the end of the season he was shooting entirely on his own.

The biggest problem from the point of view of his guests was that, delightful and friendly though he was, he had no idea how to run a shoot and he fired indiscriminately at everything.

He fired at birds that were clearly flying over the Guns on either side of him and several times he walked along the line of Guns firing at whichever birds took his fancy. This would have been bad enough but throughout the morning he swore continually. If he hit a bird the swearing was pretty bad but each time he missed it was appalling. His guests stayed the course out of politeness, but were relieved to escape at the end of the day. No one accepted any further invitations and the baffled hat maker simply assumed they were busy and carried on organising shoots entirely for his own benefit. He grew ever more eccentric and as the years went by his house became dilapidated and the few people who called noticed only that he left his furniture and pictures out on the lawns for days at a time in all weathers and was often to be seen sitting in an armchair on the lawn smoking in the pouring rain. He also took to placing hundreds of hats in the trees and shooting at them.

He then started to import exotic animals, which lived in the house or wandered in and out as they liked through doors that were always left open. It was at this stage that his housekeeper left for good. Undaunted he bought numerous monkeys, a bear and a pygmy hippopotamus, which quickly died. According to reports that began to be carried in the local newspaper he even had parts of the house demolished and simply left the rubble where it had fallen.

He took to shooting birds from his bedroom window and had a lake dug where his lawn had once been. He then shot any duck that came in to the water.

The few visitors to the house, including the postman, reported that he was immensely charming when they met him and he reportedly invited any schoolboy who wandered on to his land to fish his stream and shoot his rabbits as often as they pleased, but in the end his eccentricities got the better of him and he was arrested by the police after being found wandering in his pyjamas, gun in hand, in a nearby village.

It was only when a distant relative came to live with him and a full-time nurse was employed to look after him that people remembered he had once been a hatter. Hats were made at that time using mercury and even small amounts of mercury absorbed into the body cause odd behaviour – the more mercury, the stranger the behaviour. It seems that our eccentric shooting man really was quite literally a mad hatter!

Something's cooking

By the 1920s the English aristocracy had realised that English food really was awful. It was during this hedonistic decade, following the austerity of the Great War, that the wealthy English did everything they could to adopt the culinary style of the continent. The morals of the French were still suspect, it is true, but their food was another matter entirely as authors such as P.G.Wodehouse recognised. In *The Code of the Woosters*, for example, Bertie Wooster's greatest fear is that his Aunt's French cook will be lured away to work for another aristocrat.

In the real world this fear was, if anything, even more pronounced and one lord found a novel solution to the problem of keeping his French cook happy.

The lord in question wrote an article in the *Gentleman's Magazine* explaining how he had enticed his cook over from France by offering to let him shoot every Saturday with his other guests right through the season. It happened that, like so many of his countrymen, the cook was a fanatical shooting man and his employer had one of the best pheasant shoots in England. The lure of guaranteed sport every weekend was too much for the poor Frenchman who declined a far better paid job simply so he could have access to such good shooting.

The other Guns were very grand and rather horrified at having to shoot with someone who was so much their social inferior but the owner of the shoot was deaf to their complaints. 'I don't care if he is the lowest of the low. He cooks like an angel and he can damn well shoot all my pheasants just so long as he keeps cooking for me!'

Drinks party

Many of shooting's most famous tales centre on the highly eccentric Viscount Massereene and Ferrard who owned a fine shooting estate in County Antrim, Ireland.

The noble lord found that as he grew older his enthusiasm for shooting declined as his fondness for alcohol increased. Despite this he took a great interest in the organisation of his shoot days. He would direct that a table and chair be placed on the lawn at the front of the house first thing in the morning. Here he would sit with a row of bottles in front of him containing his favourite drinks: gin, brandy, rum and whisky. Before taking up their positions the beaters would then gather in a line leading up to the table. A servant gave each beater a number on a piece of paper.

Massereene would then begin to call out the beaters' numbers.

'Number one. What will you have?'

'I'll be quite happy with whatever your lordship chooses,' came the traditional reply.

'Brandy then,' said his lordship.

Massereene would then take the brandy bottle pour a glass and drink it himself!

'That's just right for you,' he would say before selecting another glass, filling it and handing it to the beater.

This would be repeated until all the beaters had been offered a drink and had their health drunk by the noble lord. The marvel of the thing is that by the time the beaters had all been accommodated with a drink and set off for their day's work, Lord Massereene was still able (usually) to walk back to the house unaided.

Can't stand shooting

Driven shooting was organised on a gigantic scale in Victorian and Edwardian England. At a big shoot a Gun might easily fire one thousand five hundred cartridges in a day, which meant that many Guns were extremely deaf. Some Gun noticing that they were gradually losing their hearing, gave up shooting. Others soldiered on but took avoiding action when it came to noise.

Sir Edward Guinness used regularly to bribe the keeper to ensure that he would draw the worst pegs – pegs that virtually guaranteed no birds and therefore no noisy shooting. Sir Edward loved the social side of shooting and was happy just to stand ready in a valley or on the edge of a wood. The bribed keepers of course thought he was quite mad!

Repel boarders!

The great Victorian eccentric Colonel George Hangar loved shooting, organised tremendous driven pheasant days but refused to allow anyone to shoot with him. He became so obsessed with keeping all his pheasants to himself that he employed a number of bizarre methods to keep others – but particularly poachers – at bay.

He built several massive cannons and had them fixed around the parapet of his house, which overlooked his woods. Hangar used moulded clay balls filled with marbles in his cannons and fired them off at the least sign of a disturbance – the hissing, whizzing noise as the clay balls burst and the marbles ricocheted all over the place was enough to terrify any would-be poacher.

Hangar's keepers and beaters lived in constant fear of their master's hair-brained schemes and none more so than his head keeper whose house was built with neither doors nor windows on the ground floor.

The idea was that the keeper would be safe from the attention of vengeful poachers. The keeper's reaction to having to live in a house that could only be entered using a ladder is not recorded.

The lower, windowless rooms received a dim light from windows fixed at various angles on the first floor. The idea was that, having climbed his ladder, the keeper could draw it up after him at night safe in the knowledge that any poacher would have to batter through the ground floor walls to get at him.

A walkway from the top of the house allowed the keeper to cross to a thirty-foot tower surmounted by one of Hangar's special cannons.

Shot pants

When it comes to sporting shooting safety is a relatively modern concept.

Modern Guns would be horrified at the antics of their shooting forebears who, generally speaking, took a pretty lackadaisical attitude to the dangers of guns.

A good example of how things could go badly wrong occurred in the 1860s on a small Essex shooting estate.

Lined out along a lane where a single cottage stood back a little in its own garden, the Guns were enjoying an occasional flurry of birds when the Gun nearest the garden unaccountably took a shot at a low bird. The shot was immediately followed by a cry from the cottage garden.

'Hi! You've bloomin well shot me, yer bugger.'

The wayward Gun turned pale and ran towards the cottage. He looked over the fence and saw a very old man tottering towards him. It transpired that the old man had been bending over tending to his flowerbeds when he felt his rear end being peppered with shot. More shocked than hurt he nonetheless began cursing till the air was blue.

When the old man's corduroy trousers were examined dozens of pieces of shot were discovered flattened against the cotton pile – in effect his immensely thick trousers had acted as armour plating and protected him from serious injury.

Much relieved, the offending Gun presented the old man with a guinea and vowed never to shoot from the lane again.

Bugger, it's a balloon!

The Montgolfier brothers were the first to invent a means by which humans could travel through the air high above the ground. Their first manned balloon ascent took off in June 1783 and, overnight, they became the toast of Europe.

Kites had long been used to try to direct birds on formal shoots towards the Guns but a keen-eyed Frenchman called Henri Chasteau de Ballion decided that a balloon could make shooting an even more exciting pastime than it was already. On his huge estate he had already tried to adopt the habits of the English by releasing pheasants and then trying to drive them towards the Guns. It had worked well enough, but de Ballion was always looking for something new. He had tried dozens of different shot and powder combinations in his guns, he had experimented with different bores and had even had guns specially commissioned and made to his own design in an attempt to create the ultimate sporting weapon. He'd tried 6 and 8 bores, he tried 16 and 20 bores; he tried massive fowling pieces of every conceivable size but somehow nothing quite worked as well as he thought it might even though he had no specific aim in mind. He wanted a gun that would be light and effective; a gun that was powerful and elegant, that would stop a sparrow or a rhino, but when his search for this ultimate weapon failed he decided that the solution was not the gun but the environment in which the gun was used.

When word reached him about the Montgolfiers' experiments with hot air balloons he was hugely excited. He decided to build his own. He first tried animal skins and had half his herd of prize cattle killed and flayed to provide sufficient skin. The skins were carefully stitched together but were far too heavy and the balloon failed to take to the air. Next he tried paper carefully glued together but it was too fragile and tore quickly. He tried again using the finest cloth and with a net stretched over the outside to hold the thing in shape. This time it worked and his balloon soared up to more than three hundred feet. It was let out on long ropes and when the fuel had all burned up the balloon drifted slowly back to earth.

On each of the following ten days de Ballion loaded the fuel burner, told his servants to hold the ropes and had himself let up gently into the sky. When he reached the height of the tallest trees in a distant wood he waved to the men below and the balloon was tied securely. He then sat and waited and took an occasional shot at a passing bird. It was the greatest pleasure he had ever known he later said, but after a season or two the novelty wore off and the carefully made balloon was consigned to a corner of an old barn where it gradually fell to pieces.

Fowling nightshirt

One of the greatest – and maddest – sportsmen who ever lived was the eighteenth century Shropshire landowner John Mytton. Despite enjoying the responsibilities of high office – he was High Sheriff of the county of Shropshire as well as MP for Shrewsbury for a number of years – he was addicted to shooting, hunting, practical jokes and dangerous escapades.

He was a passionate wildfowler and in the depths of winter would regularly get out of bed in the middle of the night and set off completely naked across the fields to his lake. Having shot for an hour or so he would return to his bed, get bored and then get up and return once more to the lake.

On more formal shoots he wore thin linen shirts and fine city shoes and never a coat or hat. He could never be bothered with underwear or a coat of any kind.

He was famous among the locals for driving his carriage around and throwing money out of the windows – so much so that when word got out that he was planning a journey the route would be lined with the hopeful multitude. He made numerous attempts to drive his carriage at a fence in such a way that the whole contraption would be carried safely over – but the result was always a smashed carriage. He claimed that he drank at least four bottles of port each day throughout his adult life but despite being continually drunk he was said by contemporaries to be a fine shot. Among his other eccentric habits were biting horses he didn't like, riding his pet bear in the garden and taking absurd or impossible bets. By the time he died aged just thirty-eight he had bankrupted the estate and spent what in today's values would amount to £20 million.

2 The Golden Age

Long walk

In a lifetime's shooting that ended in 1840 Lord Malmesbury reckoned he'd walked a total of 36,200 miles, or nearly one and a half times round the world, in pursuit of a total bag of 38,934. To achieve that bag he had fired 54,987 shots. Perhaps even more remarkable than these figures is the fact that Malmesbury bothered to keep such precise records, but then our Victorian sporting ancestors were nothing if not meticulous in their record keeping.

Malmesbury was just one of a number of remarkable nineteenth century shooting aristocrats. Some were famous for the numbers they shot, others for their sheer skill.

Thomas Lord Walsingham, for example and Lord Ripon were among the greatest shots who ever lived and if practice makes perfect then practice may fairly be given as among the main reasons for their extraordinary skill. With the fashion for huge numbers of birds at its height, Victorian and Edwardian England provided the perfect setting for remarkable Shots to emerge.

Lord Walsingham is credited with having shot 1070 grouse in one day using just 1510 cartridges. He twice killed three birds in the air with just one shot. He used three guns in combination with two loaders and a cartridge boy. In one day in January 1889 Walsingham shot the biggest mixed bag recorded: thirty-nine pheasants, six partridges, twenty-three mallard, six gadwall, four pochard duck, one goldeneye, seven teal, three swans, a woodcock, three snipe, a woodpigeon, two herons, sixty-five coots, two moorhens, nine hares, sixteen rabbits, an otter, a pike (which was shot as it swam through shallow water) and a rat.

Red-faced Cardigan

James Thomas Brudenell, seventh Earl of Cardigan, led the Charge of the Light Brigade at Balaclava in the Crimea in 1854. His incompetence in deciding to pit lightly armed cavalrymen against heavy Russian artillery meant that two hundred and fifty men were killed or injured out of a force of six hundred and thirty-seven.

Cardigan also invented the garment that still bears his name and he was famously arrogant. He hated to be in the wrong and believed completely in his own abilities. He was furious too if on his shoot the keepers failed to provide high, fast-flying birds whatever the weather, but despite his rages and his wealth even he occasionally failed.

While shooting one January day in the 1850s Cardigan thought that the birds were simply too few in number and rather bedraggled. Convinced he knew how to remedy the situation far better than his own keeper he summoned the hapless man and pointing to a distant copse said.

'I want you to beat through that wood.'

The keeper tried to object but his Lordship was having none of it: 'Not a word, sir.'

The keeper set off with his beaters and began the drive from the wood. It produced a huge number of high flying birds and Cardigan was delighted.

Later in the day he took great pleasure in pointing out to the keeper that he had been right all along.

The keeper waited until his employer had finished boasting to his fellow Guns about his knowledge of driving birds and then said in a low voice:

'But my lord, I questioned your decision so far as that wood was concerned for the simple reason that it isn't your wood. It's your neighbour's!'

Record breaker

Today we tend to frown on driven pheasant shoots that go for huge numbers rather than smaller quantities of really good birds. In the past big bags were far more fashionable and various shoots competed for the record.So far as anyone can tell the biggest bag of game ever shot in one day in Britain was at Hall Barn Beaconsfield, Buckinghamshire on the Burtley Beat on 18 December 1913.

George V, the Prince of Wales, Lord Charles Fitzmaurice, Lord Ilchester, Lord Dalhousie, Lord Herbert Vane-Tempest and the Hon H. Stonor shot a staggering 3937 pheasants, three partridges, four rabbits and one various (probably a pigeon) making a total of 3945.

Other huge bags included one made at Water Priory, Yorkshire on the Golden Valley beat on 5 December 1909 when nine guns – all dukes and earls shot 3824 pheasants, 15 partridges, 526 hares, 92 rabbits and three various for a total of 4460. The following day the same team reached a total of three thousand pheasants by lunchtime when high winds forced them to call a halt.

Outside the UK Count Louis Karolyi's estate at Totmeyer, Hungary is said to have organised a day's shooting on which 6125 pheasants were shot along with 150 hares and fifty partridges.

Other huge bags include nearly seven thousand rabbits in one day at Blenheim Palace in Oxfordshire on 7 October 1898.

More than half a century earlier, on 26 October 1826, at Whittlesea

Mere in Cambridgeshire Colonel Peter Hawker recorded 504 starlings killed using nearly two pounds of shot in his double punt gun. Hawker reckoned his personal lifetime bag at three million head of game – unquestionably a gross exaggeration. His total was, however, still enormous by modern standards – probably in the region of eighteen to twenty thousand head of game

Complete bustard

Wilton House and its owner Lord Pembroke provided seemingly endless shooting parties for the titled and rich. His Monday to Thursday parties at the end of the ninetenth century, often included foreign heads of state in addition to the usual earls and dukes and on one occasion he found himself host to the German ambassador.

The ambassador had little knowledge of the traditions of driven shooting but he had a reputation as a fine shot. From the very first drive however, it was apparent that the ambassador was a disaster when it came to safety and etiquette – he constantly shot low birds, poached his neighbours' birds, took pot shots at birds that were clearly out of range and kept shooting after the beaters had come into view.

Lord Pembroke was aghast. As the day progressed things went from bad to worse and the ambassador shot ever more wildly – he peppered several beaters, two of his fellow guests and a dog. No one was badly hurt but the ambassador seemed blithely unaware that he had done anything wrong.

By the end of the day Pembroke's guests told him they would not shoot at all the next day if the ambassador were allowed to take part.

How could the ambassador be got rid of without offending him and causing a diplomatic row? Pembroke had the answer. The ambassador had enquired about a great bustard in a glass case in the hall. The species was extinct locally but Lord Pembroke told the ambassador that if he liked he could go in pursuit of bustard the following day. The ambassador was delighted at the prospect but was told that the tradition of shooting bustard in England meant he would have to shoot on his own.

Off the ambassador went in the morning on a heavily laden pack pony and in the direction of Salisbury plain. Meanwhile Pembroke's other guests set off for a day of unmolested shooting.

Back at the house that evening Pembroke found the ambassador in a foul mood. 'I have had a dreadful day,' he said, 'I have walked miles across foul empty countryside and what do I have to show for it – just three of these damned bustards of yours!'

Two in the air

Trick shooting was enormously popular among Victorians. Their enthusiasm for shots over the shoulder and shots between the legs deepened as clay shooting became ever more popular and as news of the prowess of American sportsmen and women – including the famous Annie Oakley – filtered across the Atlantic.

Colonel Peter Hawker, who was fascinated by shooting of every variety, once visited Lord Portsmouth's estate after hearing about the remarkable trick-shooting abilities of a local keeper.

Mr Ford the keeper had developed an extraordinary ability – he was able to put his cocked and loaded gun on the ground, throw two pennies into the air and then pick the gun up quickly enough to hit one penny with each barrel before they came back down to earth.

Hawker tried repeatedly to master this particular trick but with no success – indeed he claimed that he never saw any other gun match Ford's speed and accuracy.

World's worst shot?

The sixth Duke of Devonshire was famous for his wealth, his ancient lineage and his appalling shooting! It was said of him that he was more likely to hit a target if he tried to miss it than if he made any attempt to aim at it. But he was an enormous optimist and despite staggering levels of incompetence he never stopped trying.

He came close to disaster on a number of occasions and none more so than when with one shot he managed to wound a pheasant along with the dog that was chasing it, the picker-up and an innocent bystander. His friends supported him through thick and thin and when he hit a very high partridge while shooting at Cresswell Crags there were loud cheers. His Grace was baffled as he'd actually fired at a pheasant and missed!

Donkey rides

One of the greatest pleasures of the traditional shooting day is lunch and for many lunch meant the chance to talk, to gossip about one's friends and their doings.

Lord Alvanley and Lord de Ros were great shooting friends and inveterate gossips as well as practical jokers. If one of their jokes worked it often became the staple of shooting lunch conversations for months, even years, afterwards. The two friends were also keen gambling men who would bet on anything and everything.

Out rough shooting one day de Ros suggested to Alvanley that it might be amusing to if they each agreed to carry whatever the other shot. A little later de Ros spotted a donkey and promptly shot it. Lord Alvanley's reaction is not recorded!

Bad beaters

Beaters are the unsung heroes of driven shooting and should be treated with the greatest respect. In Victorian England they were often neglected or treated as inferior beings. Occasionally they had their revenge. On some shoots it was traditional for the beaters to wear white smocks of the kind worn by eighteenth Century shepherds. On one shoot the owner decided that each beater's smock should have a big black-painted letter – from A through to Z – on the back to make it easier to identify each man.

Understandably the beaters felt rather humiliated by their smock labels and they began to grumble. Outright rebellion was impossible so they began a campaign of what today might be called passive resistance. The highlight of the campaign came when a group of Guns and their wives were enjoying lunch on the lawn in front of the house. The beaters were some way off with their back to them when someone noticed that as if by chance the beaters had sat in such a way that the letters on their backs spelled out some extremely rude words. The smocks and letters were quickly abandoned.

Lightly poached

Venison has always commanded high prices so it is no surprise that poachers have long targeted the Highlands of Scotland, and policing this vast and remote area has always been difficult, but occasionally the authorities get lucky.

On one such occasion a team of keepers saw a distant stag suddenly collapse. Then came the report of a rifle. This was not the stalking season so the keepers ran quickly towards the spot where they'd last seen the stag, then they waited. The minutes passed, then the hours but no one appeared to collect the stag.

It grew dark and still the keepers waited. They organised shifts so the men could wait and rest alternately. Two keepers were posted on a nearby track.

By the light of an almost full moon they watched and waited and it was only when the first glimmerings of dawn appeared that they saw a figure approaching from a great distance.

When he was within sixty or seventy feet of the dead deer he began to do something quite extraordinary. He started picking up large stones and hurling them at the carcase. As the rocks and stones rained down around the deer it was only a matter of time before one of the waiting keepers was hit. The stone hit him a glancing blow but it was enough to make him cry out and no sooner had he done so than the stone throwing poacher ran in the opposite direction as fast as his legs would carry him.

The keepers leapt from the hiding place and set off in hot pursuit but within a few hundred yards the poacher had vanished into an impenetrable area of scrub and trees and his pursuers soon realised they would never find him. They walked slowly back to the deer thinking that at least the poacher had failed to collect the venison. Imagine their horror when they discovered that the deer had vanished. The decoy poacher had drawn them away leaving the coast clear for his accomplice to pick up the deer.

Waterton's fakery

Charles Waterton (1782-1865) was one of Britain's most eccentric landowners. As a young man he had travelled widely in South America where he is said to have hunted caiman by holding a knife between his teeth and then jumping on their backs.

Back in England he inherited the family's huge estate in Yorkshire and immediately built a high wall around all his land. The wall ran for more than ten miles and was so expensive to build that he was almost bankrupted.

Having been a keen sportsman he decided he no longer enjoyed shooting pheasants and rabbits. Instead he organised rat shoots – this was the only animal he decided he no longer liked.

He began to pay the local villagers to bring him live hedgehogs and hares, which he released in his own grounds. He spent much of each day – particularly in summer – perched high in one of his trees trying to tame the song birds and get them to eat from his hand.

When poachers began regularly to invade his estate he sat out all night firing regularly into the air to deter them and when that didn't work he had hundreds of wooden pheasant silhouettes made and nailed them up in trees all over the estate. Since the poachers always came at night and relied on spotting birds silhouetted against the sky they ended up wasting their shots – so much so that they quickly gave up and Waterton was able to return to his rat shoots and tree climbing.

His biggest contribution to sporting shooting was the development of new ways of preserving animals – he was a brilliant taxidermist, but his prolific use of a number of dangerous chemicals may have led to his increasing eccentricity. When guests occasionally came for dinner – and their presence was an increasing rarity as he grew older – he would hang upside down from a door and talk to them while he ate. At night he slept on the floor with a wooden pillow under his head and his clothes became so threadbare that on several occasions he was mistaken for a tramp and had pennies pressed into his hand, a circumstance which delighted him.

Top shot

Shooting at his huge estate at Zidlochovice in the Czech Republic a little over a century ago the Hapsburg King Carol is reputed to have killed in a single day eight hundred and thirty three pheasants.

In the days before pump action and repeater shotguns he was able to achieve this extraordinary score only by using a team of three highly experienced loaders. Assuming he was a better than average shot, that total of birds must have meant he fired at least fifteen hundred cartridges.

Chicken shooting

In 1963 Lord Home of the Hirsel renounced his numerous titles (including an earldom) to become plain Sir Alec Douglas Home so that he could serve as Prime Minister. He had served in several of the great offices of state before becoming Prime Minister and he never lost his love for public life, but throughout his years in the House of Commons and the House of Lords he also never lost his love for fishing and shooting, especially at his ancestral home at the Hirsel on the Scottish borders. Home was a fund of good shooting stories and among the best was his tale of the enthusiastic Shot who once visited the Hirsel.

When the man arrived Home politely asked if his guest would like to try the grouse shooting on the estate. The visitor was enthusiastic but confessed he had absolutely no experience or knowledge of grouse. His sole concern seemed to be to establish exactly how big these grouse were. He was keen, he said, to shoot something substantial.

The next morning Home, ever the good host, put his visitor in the best butt on the moors, the butt over which the bulk of the best birds usually flew. It was a wonderful morning and shooting from a butt further down the line Home was sure things were going well for all the Guns.

At the lunch he gently enquired if his guest had enjoyed the morning. 'There was nothing to shoot,' came the visitor. 'I saw only dozens of poultry, some kind of chicken I think they must have been.' Clearly for this particular Shot, size really mattered!

Best shot ever?

The Victorian Tommy de Grey, who was to become the sixth Lord Walsingham, was passionate about shooting to the point of obsession. He and his friend and rival Lord de Grey vied for the title best shot ever throughout most of their adult lives.

Walsingham's greatest claim to fame is that in one day at Blubberhouses Moor in Yorkshire he shot more than one thousand grouse. This was partly made possible by the fact that Blubberhouses is shaped roughly like an hour glass and Walsingham positioned himself in the narrowest part, the bottleneck through which the birds would be funnelled but he still had to hit them and few would dispute the extraordinary brilliance with which he did this.

Walsingham was a dazzlingly quick shot too, particularly when breech-loading guns began to be used but even with black powder and muzzle-loading guns he was fast – provided he was accompanied by his trusty expert loaders.

During the days when black powder and muzzleloaders were still in use Walsingham and de Grey frequently shot together. On one famous occasion de Grey saw Walsingham shooting at his usual incredible pace when suddenly he seemed to catch fire and a for a dazzling moment de Grey saw Walsingham illuminated like a flaming torch while carrying on shooting as if nothing had happened.

What caused the conflagration was a small spill of black power on to the butt of one of Walsingham's guns. Somehow this was ignited just at the moment it was shaken off the butt onto to Walsingham's shoulder. Though it looked like his lordship was on fire for a moment it seems he was, in the event, only slighted singed.

Rapid fire with a difference

An elderly and very eccentric Yorkshire landowner had become increasingly reclusive. His family had ceased to visit him for the simple reason that he was so rude to them when they called. He had no friends and seemed to relish his increasing isolation. He had several thousand acres of land on which there were game-filled woods as well as a long stretch of trout-filled river.

As the years went by he gave up farming and caring for his woodland and relied on his enormous investments to keep him going. But he grew ever more passionate about his shooting and fishing and spent almost every day either wandering the field with his gun at the ready or catching endless trout and grayling from his river.

His keeper, one of the few men to whom he ever spoke, later reported that, in his last years, the old man had become ever more eccentric. In summer he insisted on fishing his river while swimming in it without a stitch of clothing on and in the shooting season he ordered his men to load a dozen or more shotguns and then prop them in a line in a specially built rack. He would then order his beaters to go into action and as the birds flew over he would run along the line of loaded guns, pick one out, fire it and then hurl it on the ground behind him before reaching for the next gun. Once the twelve guns had been fired he blew a loud whistle and his beaters stopped advancing until all twelve guns had been re-loaded and he was ready to resume shooting.

Throughout this bizarre operation he would swear and curse under his breath and at the end of the day with as many as a hundred pheasants ready to be picked up he would instruct his keeper to leave them to rot where they fell as the taste and sight of pheasant disgusted him!

Deer me

Stalking, far more than pheasant shooting or grouse shooting, is very much the sport of kings.

The Victorian sportsman and writer Charles St John had shot hundreds of stags in his career when he set off, filled with confidence, one autumn morning in pursuit of a particularly fine stag. Like all stalkers he knew that the real skill in stalking is not in the shooting but in getting close enough for a shot without spooking the animal.

After what seemed like hours St John was well positioned to take his shot. It was a difficult shot because only the stag's head and neck were visible but St John squeezed the trigger and the stag instantly collapsed – only to get up almost immediately and run off!

St John moved quickly in the stag's direction. The beast had staggered away up the hill but now turned and headed directly towards St John. It reached a burn that separated man from beast and then collapsed again. St John assumed it was now dead and grabbed its horns ready to pull it out of the burn. Suddenly with no warning the stag came back to life and launched a frenzied attack on the astonished stalker. St John was kicked and buffeted by the stag which, having knocked him down, then tried to stamp on him. St John hit his head so hard that for a few moments he was unconscious. He'd dropped his gun and his only way to escape was up the steep side of the burn – he scrambled away with the enraged stag just a few feet behind. There then followed a curious few minutes during which the man and the stag faced each other across the burn. Neither moved and St John knew that if the stag didn't die soon he might well be injured or even killed. Then St John decided he had to do something – he still had a tartan rug round his shoulders and hardly thinking what he was doing he leapt at the stag and threw his rug over its head. The stag collapsed under the weight, but then recovered and bucked and kicked with the stalker still hanging on for dear life. St John confessed later that he'd felt such pity for the poor beast and such shame about his bungled shot that he almost decided there are then to give up stalking.

Meanwhile the stag seemed to have lost none of its energy and the last thing St John remembered was being thrown by a particularly strong toss of the stag's head. He fell to the ground and when he woke several minutes later he found himself alone and suffering only from a few bad scratches and bruises. The stag, by now very dead indeed, lay just a few yards away.

Good tip for the keeper

A century ago argument raged in the press and on the great (and not so great) estates over the ticklish problem of tipping keepers and beaters.

A case related in *The Times* newspaper in 1898 revealed something of the difficulties.

'A gentleman was invited to shoot in Scotland at two places close together. He arrived at the first place and immediately after his arrival received a telegram calling him back to town. He, however, determined to have one day's shooting and to proceed to town by the night mail. At the end of the day he gave the head-keeper £1 and asked him to send his gun and cartridge-bag over to the other place for which he had an invitation, and where he proposed proceeding in three or four days' time. On his arrival there after his visit to town he found his gun, etc, had not arrived, whereupon he wrote to the keeper asking him to forward it at once, and he received a reply stating that when he, the keeper, had received the other £4 to which he was entitled the gun would be forwarded: meantime it was detained till payment was made. The gentleman wrote to the keeper's master and received a reply that he, the master, never interfered between his guests and his servants in the matter of tips. The gentleman ascertained that the master in question paid the keeper no wages, but left him to get what he could out of the guests.'

Highly trained

The great age of the railway – the boom years of the mid-nineteenth century – gave a number of very rich men the chance to own their own, full size train sets. Several landowners paid for the railway companies to extend their lines on to particular estates, one or two aristocrats became passionate amateur drivers and at least one landowner was eccentric enough to build himself a railway specifically to get from one drive to the next on his pheasant shoot!

It is true that the drives were widely spaced and the landowner was elderly but the horse-drawn game cart and several specially adapted carriages had done the job well enough for decades. But this particular landowner loved the idea of steam and since he had the money to indulge his fantasy he went ahead and built a couple of miles of railway. He called in the teams of engineers and within a few months he had a miniature railway built complete with open carriages painted in his favourite colours. He learned to drive the train and persuaded the bemused engineers to build the track so it ran from one drive to the next, even taking in odd bits of woodland on the edges of the estate that were driven only now and then. He also made sure that a switchback section led into his favourite wood for roost shooting pigeon. The result was a great success and on formal days the landowner had the great pleasure of personally driving his guests from drive to drive and then back to the house for lunch.

3 Wild about Wildfowl

Goose surprise

Anyone who has read the famous children's story *Little Grey Men* or the wildfowling classic *Tide's Ending* will know the writer BB whose real name was Denys Watkins-Pitchford. BB was a life-long devotee of wildfowling – from childhood to old age he never missed a season even when he was ill. But what BB really loved about wildfowling was not the shooting – it was the atmosphere of wild places and the chance to bag something for the pot. He disliked driven pheasant shooting but loved the isolation and remoteness of the marsh.

BB was also a keen naturalist who was fascinated by the lives of wild creatures. So much so that at various times in his life he kept wild birds and young foxes, but his most bizarre animal acquisition was his pet goose. This much loved goose almost ended up in the cooking pot and the story of how it avoided that fate is remarkable and typical of BB's delightfully eccentric ways.

The story begins on the Wash in Lincolnshire, a place of lonely, dangerous mudflats and rip tides that cut off the unwary in seconds; a place where no fowler would dare go without a local guide. Without local knowledge the mudflats can be treacherous and many shooters have lost their lives in this unforgiving terrain.

BB always took a guide although he probably knew the Wash as well as any outsider. He was shooting in the early morning hoping to catch the geese on their dawn flight. He'd watched the light grow in intensity until, almost imperceptibly, the details round about became clear and it was morning. Then he heard the unmistakable sound of the geese coming towards him. Looking up he saw they were well within range. He fired, bringing one of the trailing geese down well behind him. The bird was only winged and by the time BB caught up with it the goose, which was a big one, was in a very bad mood. It didn't try to run off, but with one wing clearly broken it merely looked at BB and charged at him. Under other circumstances BB might have grabbed it and simply knocked it on the head or if it had been able to run he might have had another shot at it.

For some reason this time he didn't. He was never really able to explain why, but he made a grab at the bird and tucked it under one arm. He carried the goose back to the car and took it home where he nursed it for several weeks. The bird made a complete recovery and became one of BB's greatest friends. It lived for many years and was by far the best guard dog BB ever had – at least that was his story.

Near miss

The demise of punt gunning has long been predicted but the sport somehow manages to survive – by a whisker. In former times punt gunners made a living by shooting large numbers of wildfowl and waders and sending them to the London markets.

The gunners' punts were canoe-like, but much longer and designed to sit as low in the water as possible to avoid being seen by the birds. The gunner would lie face down in the punt with his massive punt gun running from the centre of the punt forward right along the bow to project a foot or more out over the end of the boat and just above the water. A tiny scull in each hand would be used gradually to manoeuvre the punt within range and then the massive gun would be fired.

As with stalking the real skill lay in getting within range of a raft of birds and the idea was to bring down as many birds as possible for this was effectively commercial shooting.

Towards the end of the great days of punt gunning a few rather grand public school boy amateurs – such as the naturalist Sir Peter Scott – took up the sport, but they never really learned the instinctive skills of the locals. Punt gunning was and is a dangerous sport and many an amateur has vanished while out on the water. Even local experts sometimes got into trouble as one old gunner recalled at the end of the nineteenth century.

He and a companion were out on a high tide knowing that a large party of grey geese had recently arrived. The two gunners decided to work their way slowly toward where they thought the birds were, each in their separate punts but always keeping an eye out for the other. When the old man gave the signal they would fire their guns.

'All went well at first, but we got separated in the end of it, but I knew he must be pretty close by all the while as I could sense the line of the sand and I could hear the geese talking at the edge of it. There they sat gabbling and splashing though I couldn't quite see them. Then I made out a body of them to the right, so I backed my paddle and looked along my big gun to see how to take them. They seemed a bit too quiet for geese. Then I thought maybe it was a piece of wreck, but I couldn't see any break in the line of it. But I saw it move so I thought to myself here goes and got ready to fire. Then part of a cloud cleared off from the moon and there lay his punt with him in it. Another two seconds and I should have killed or sunk him. But for the cloud there's no doubt I would have fired. Instead I backed my other paddle, backed away and breathed a sigh. I never had such a close thing again.'

Short-un

Short-un Page was born of a long line of wildfowlers. His family had to catch eels, shoot rabbits and harvest wild geese and ducks to keep body and soul together at a time when jobs were pretty much non-existent and social security benefits unheard of.

Short-un helped his father, a professional wildfowler, from his earliest childhood, but at the age of about sixteen he decided to go it alone. He took off in his father's punt one icy day in 1953 and headed for the geese. His father's 10ft long flintlock puntgun that carried nearly five ounces of shot was aboard. From the first, Short-un seemed to lead a charmed life – with his first shot he claimed five geese. Shot number two brought him five curlew and his final shot, at the end of a day that left his hands so numb they would barely move, killed 150 waders and five wigeon. It was an astonishing beginning, but what the locals really remembered was Short-un's face when he returned home through the village that day – his face was covered with blood because, like all the old puntgunners, he killed wounded birds by crushing their skulls in his teeth!

No ordinary greylag

The writer Charles McInnes spent years trying to shoot a particular greylag goose on the Tay estuary. McInnes called it the White Queen – and he was so determined to shoot it that for years he neglected job, family, health and hygiene in pursuit of his obsession.

He hardly bothered with the other kinds of shooting that had once entranced him and almost drowned on several occasions so desperate were his attempts to get within range of the elusive greylag. He often saw the white goose, but somehow she was always a little too far away or he was in the wrong place at the wrong time.

Then towards the end of the fourth year of his pursuit, McInnes saw the White Queen flying steadily towards the ditch where he lay in wait. But having been momentarily elated McInnes' spirits fell as he saw the great bird begin to veer away. McInnes couldn't bear to lose her again so he took a chance on a long shot and fired. To his astonishment the white goose faltered and then fell.

But then McInnes realised what a terrible mistake he'd made for the great white bird had fallen into the sea and the tide was racing. He threw his gun and bag to the ground and began to ran along the mudflats desperately trying to keep pace with her, then he plunged into the freezing sea wading through the water until he became stuck fast in mud up to his waist. He watched helplessly as the bird drifted away. McInnes had all the benefits of a formidable physique and after a few frightening moments he managed to pull himself out of the mud – minus his boots. He still refused to give up and immediately set off along the mud following the direction of the goose which he could just about see out on the water. Having caught up with the drifting bird he stripped off completely, dived in and began swimming out to sea – and this in temperatures below freezing.

He reached a sandbank and saw the bird just a dozen or so feet out to sea but on the wrong side of the sandbank. There was nothing he could do so he stood virtually naked and watched as his prize goose moved gently out to sea. He waited till it was out of sight. He returned to shore and on the verge of hypothermia got back into his clothes before stumbling to a nearby farmhouse. He was lucky to be alive. For the rest of his life he regretted he hadn't taken a dog.

Fowl up

Wildfowling was and is one of Britain's most dangerous sports. It is not the shotguns that cause the problems but rather the remote places where wildfowlers enjoy their sport.

A copy of a long vanished Norfolk newspaper published in 1900 records a story that almost led to the death of a wildfowler – in fact the story is a reminder of the perils of shooting on mudflats at low tide where even the most experienced shot can get into serious difficulties.

The paper records that the fowler had set off early in the morning to a stretch of foreshore where he had shot regularly for years. What the fowler hadn't realised was that work on a number of sea defences further up the coast had changed the mud landscape.

Several freezing hours later he had bagged a couple of mallard and decided to call it a day. He began the long march back across the sticky mud knowing that he had at least thirty minutes safety margin before his retreat would be cut off by the incoming tide. But he had reckoned without those changes up the coast. He reached a gulley that would normally have been dry at this time of day and was horrified to discover deep swirling water cutting him off from the distant sand dunes.

He ran wildly along the edge of the gulley ever more desperate and seeing no way to cross the water that was rising higher with every passing second.

Then on the distant sandy shore he saw a Labrador. He shouted and waved, hoping that the Labrador might attract the attention of his owner but instead the dog simply stopped and stared across at him. This went on for some time but then the dog did something extraordinary. It plunged into the water and began swimming towards the stranded fowler. A few minutes later it clambered up the side of the muddy gully, shook itself and began nuzzling his leg.

The stranded fowler stared back across the gully hoping to catch a glimpse of the dog's owner, but the beach and distant dunes were deserted.

The dog began to whine and looked as if it wanted to get back to the shore. Whenever the fowler ignored it, the dog began to whine. By now there was little chance of surviving long enough in the water to make the shore if he risked dying of cold by swimming, but his other options had all vanished. Then he had an idea. He left his gun and bag, his boots and cartridge bag and his heavy waterproofs on the ground and walked to the edge of the gully with the dog. He grabbed its collar and urged it into the water. Within seconds the dog was pulling strongly for the shore with the wildfowler hanging on to its collar and kicking with his legs as hard as he could. But the water was so cold that within a minute he had become completely numb; he began to feel sleepy and was in danger of giving up so terrible was the cold. But each time his determination flagged the dog barked loudly as if willing him to keep trying. Moments later they reached the beach and the wildfowler was able to stagger half a mile to the nearest house. Without the help of the dog he would certainly have died but when he had dried himself, warmed up and was ready to head for home he asked the couple who had helped him if they had seen the dog that had accompanied him. They shook their heads and told him he had been alone when he reached their cottage. He never discovered who owned the dog and he never saw it again.

Goose watch

The Victorian sportsman John Guille Millais – a relative of the great pre-Raphaelite painter – was a brilliant naturalist who made some unique observations of greylag geese on Loch Leven. Like most wildfowlers he may have been keen to shoot geese but he was also fascinated by their lifestyle.

Rather than simply lie out on the marsh hiding behind a wall or waiting in a gully for the birds to fly overhead Millais decided to apply science to the business of ambush. He decided to dig a pit to hide in. He covered it with muddy branches and other scraps to make it indistinguishable from the rest of the foreshore and early one morning he settled down to wait. What he saw over the next two hours had never been observed before and though it had little to do directly with shooting, Millais would not have been in a position to notice it had he not been out with his gun.

A single goose came winging in from the distance, but rather than make its way directly overhead the bird carefully quartered the ground as if checking that all was well and no danger lurked. Having given the whole area a careful once-over the goose departed back the way it had come and without once alighting.

Fascinated, Millais forgot all about his gun and simply watched through a tiny gap in his camouflage roof. A few moments after the goose had departed a small party of half a dozen geese gradually appeared high up on the distant horizon. Like the lone goose they checked over the ground flying this way and that before swinging back round and returning the way they'd come. A few minutes later the sky was filled with geese.

The early birds had obviously returned to the main flock and indicated to them that all was apparently well. Without hesitating the huge flock circled once and landed all about Millais who remained carefully concealed in his hide, hardly daring to breathe.

Immediately they landed all the geese began to feed except for six birds evenly distributed around the edge of the rough circle of geese. After ten minutes, a feeding goose walked over to one of the sentries and tapped it on the back with its beak. Immediately, the goose that had been on the look out began feeding and the other goose took over sentry duty. And so it continued as the geese took turn and turn about feeding and watching. But despite all their precautions the geese had missed the lone gunner. Having got himself in position Millais thought he ought to try a shot so he simply stood up and poked his head out through the top of his pit. He later wrote that the roar of goose wing beats that followed was almost terrifying in its intensity. Indeed so great was the noise that despite firing both barrels Millais failed to hit a single bird!

Wildfowler's wisecrack

For the great Victorian sportsman Sir Ralph Payne Gallwey shooting was a way of life and he distilled a lifetime's experience in the field into one of the great shooting books of the nineteenth century. *High Pheasants in Theory and Practice* tried to turn a sport into a science. *Letters to Young Shooters* published in three volumes was a bestseller when it first came out and is still occasionally read today which is more than can be said for most Victorian shooting books.

Payne Gallway was a great eccentric who loved practical jokes and was by all accounts a great wit. While travelling by train to the Wash with a mass of shooting equipment he met a woman who joined the train at a country station and proceeded to sit right next to him. Payne Gallwey thought of himself as a bit of a ladies man and he liked to talk to strangers.

Despite his best efforts at conversation, this particular woman refused to say a single word, which meant Payne Gallwey had to suffer a very boring journey. He was so fed up that he fell asleep. He woke a little later to discover that the woman had also fallen asleep. As he got off the train

an hour or so later he noticed that his travelling companion had woken up. Doffing his hat to her Payne Gallwey said 'Madam we might not have enjoyed much conversation, but at least we can say we have slept together.'

Sand grouse season

An old inn on the north Norfolk coast, The Cockle has long since closed but it was once the favourite haunt of a curious old wildfowler called Mr Capps.

Capps was a professional wildfowler who shot geese and duck for the London markets not for sport. He turned up regularly at The Cockle where he would offer all and sundry a sip from his hip flask. This was in the 1870s, when Norfolk was subject to occasional invasions of sand grouse – an oriental visitor that is rarely seen now. An acquaintance asked Capps to see if he could bag a couple of sand grouse for his collection.

Normally Capps would not have dreamt of trying to shoot these birds as it was out of season. But his friend was persuasive and offered Capps a rich reward for bagging the birds so Capps set off early one morning in his punt. He was not the sort of man to be embarrassed even when he was breaking the law so he was quite open about what he was up to and had spoken openly of it in The Cockle the night before. By mid-morning everyone round about knew of Capps' expedition including Mr Banks the village bobby, who decided to arrest Capps as soon as he came ashore.

Banks knew that Capps would eventually come to The Cockle Inn or into the village so he called in for a drink and to await the arrival of the sand grouse gunner. The landlord knew that trouble was brewing and he didn't want Capps arrested on the premises – partly because it would be bad for business and partly because he liked Capps who was a good customer. So he sent his wife out the back door and down to the beach half a mile away where Capps was sure to come ashore. She was to warn him and persuade him to give her the birds while he carried on up the creek into the village and The Cockle Inn.

Capps would have none of this. He'd bagged a couple of sand grouse and he was proud of it. He paddled up the creek, tied up and walked straight into The Cockle with the sand grouse swinging from his hand. The village bobby was sitting reading a newspaper and had a half empty tankard of beer in front of him.

Capps threw the birds down in front of the constable who spluttered out: 'Do you know that these are sand grouse and that it is illegal to shoot them?'

Before he could say another word Capps bellowed out 'Do you know it is against regulations to be drinking in a public house in a policeman's uniform while on duty?' Capps escorted the thunderstruck policeman into the street and shut the door behind him.

Dog gone

Shooting just wouldn't be the same without a dog. Out on the marsh or at a peg on a pheasant drive, a dog is a partner in the shooting process as well as being an excellent companion. For many shooting men life without a dog is unthinkable.

The Victorian writer John Guille Millais was often far more interested in the antics of his shooting dog than in the shooting for which he'd bought the dog in the first place. This passion for all things canine reached dizzying heights after one extraordinary day on the Tay.

Millais had downed a goose that crashed into the sea. His dog launched itself into the icy waves in pursuit. The dog vanished into the frozen distance and it took Millais some time even to locate it using his telescope. Millais grew increasingly concerned as the tiny distant dot began to fade from view. He ran along the foreshore desperately looking for a boat and after about a mile was lucky enough to come across a bait digger prepared to part with his boat for half an hour – in return for a fee.

Rowing through the blinding, freezing spray cannot have been easy but Millais was nothing if not determined and he refused to give up even as the shore began to recede and still no sign of his beloved dog. A good way out in the estuary he shouted and called to the dog but there was no response. Then he spotted a tiny black head in the distance. By now he was a mile out. He was astonished to discover his dog still carrying the heavy goose he'd shot and refusing to drop it despite the impossibility of getting back to shore. She was quite clearly prepared to die rather than give up and one can only imagine Millais' delight when he finally pulled her into the boat – still refusing to let go of the goose.

4 Nothing to Grouse About

Kamikaze grouse

Grouse shooting is not usually considered a dangerous sport but occasionally something completely unexpected happens even on the best-regulated moor. For one grouse shooter the unexpected turned into the completely extraordinary.

He was shooting on a well-known moor in Yorkshire in the early 1930s. The morning had gone well and he was waiting for another drive to begin when he spotted a lone grouse heading towards him. He watched the grouse until it seemed to disappear into a small valley a few hundred yards in front of him.

But it hadn't disappeared at all and a moment later his gun was almost wrenched out of his hand. The grouse had crashed into the barrels and lay stone dead in the butt at his feet.

Tables turned

Hunting lions and elephants was a dangerous Victorian obsession that often led to the death, not of the animal, but rather of the man in pursuit of it, but for a small bird like a grouse to go on the attack is rather more rare.

The nineteenth century writer Richard Erskine Hill once experienced an astonishing attack by a grouse that was clearly determined to get its revenge for being shot at.

He waited expectantly in his butt and as the birds began to come towards him his excitement grew. The tiny specks could be seen against the distant purple of the hills, one or two Guns had already taken a shot at early arrivals, tension was mounting.

Then suddenly he was distracted by the sight of a hare sitting just a couple of dozen yards away from him and directly ahead. He was brought back to his senses by the sharp report of two gunshots to his left.

Immediately out of the corner of his eye he saw two grouse hurtling overhead. More grouse came and then at last two were heading his way He fired at the first bird, turned to fire at the second and was instantly knocked to his feet by something that hit him very hard on the side of the head.

Dazed, he picked himself up and noticed blood steadily dripping on to the barrels of his gun. His face was covered with blood. Immediately he thought he must have been hit by a few stray pellets

At the end of the drive his fellow Guns hurried over to see what was the matter.

'That's a nasty looking eye. You'll have to have it stitched.' The speaker then glanced down at the floor of the butt and noticed a dead grouse.

'Here's the culprit!' he announced.

The bird Erskine-Hill had shot had hit him back – and hard. The grouse had been travelling so fast that it had knocked Erskine-Hill out cold.

Chance meeting

Like all sports, shooting has its fair share of remarkable coincidences. But you'd be pushed to find a more remarkable shot than one reported in the *Hexham Courier* around 1900.

A local farmer had been out rough shooting on a patch of ground with which he was as familiar as he was with his own farmyard. As the light failed he decided to push the dog through a little patch of cover by the side of a stream, a tributary of the Tyne. He spotted a covey of partridges on the far side of the stream but within range.

As soon as they saw him approach the covey got up in a great flurry and he fired both barrels as they rose. At that very moment two salmon leapt from the fast water of the stream. The farmer was so astonished that he slipped and fell to the ground killing a hare in the process. Meanwhile the shot from his two barrels had killed both salmon in mid air as well as five of the partridges in the covey.

The eyes have it

August the Twelfth. The Glorious Twelfth. For those who shoot, that date is likely always to retain its magic despite the fact that driven grouse shooting is expensive and practised in only a few areas of the North of England and Scotland.

But on one Glorious Twelfth back in the 1920s things didn't go according to plan for at least one Gun.

The party arrived early at the butts. All were vastly experienced at this sort of shooting, but rather elderly. The keeper knew each man well and knew that, in spite of their age, they were all competent shots. The morning was a great success with very fast flying birds coming steadily over the Guns. They'd been shooting well, but with one exception. One man put his gun up on numerous occasions but hardly ever fired despite the numerous birds that flew over his butt. The keepers were baffled.

Then just before lunch, the same man who had hardly fired a shot began firing almost continually even when there were no birds.

In between shots he shouted, 'Got him!' or 'Mark that bird!'. Then there would be a pause of several minutes before another rapid burst of firing none of it seemingly related to the presence (or absence) of birds in the air. They delicately asked him at lunch if they could get him anything, but he said he was fine. It was only later that the explanation for his extraordinary behaviour emerged.

It seems that a spider had attached itself to the peak of the old man's hat. It had then lowered itself from a thread until it was suspended in front of his right eye. Every time he caught sight of it he assumed it was a grouse way out in front of him and started firing!

Black grouse bonanza

Black grouse have always been relatively rare in Wales. Numbers have picked up in recent years but back in the 1920s it was rare to see a black grouse in the Principality let alone get the chance to shoot one, which makes the story of Arwel Morgan even more extraordinary.

Morgan was out shooting rabbits near Anglesey and despite walking a dozen or so miles had bagged only a couple of pigeon. He was about to start for home when he noticed a rabbit standing alert on a distant grassy knoll. He spent ten minutes taking a wide detour in the hope of getting within shooting range of the rabbit. Peering over a bush at the spot where he now thought the rabbit – or any of its fellows should be – he cursed his luck. It had vanished and yet another stalk had proved fruitless. He stood up and was about to lower the hammers on his old gun when he slipped, fell sideways and fired both barrels.

This was clearly not going to be his day so he decided to head for home. As he crossed some open ground not one hundred feet from where he'd fallen he found two black grouse stone dead and still warm. He was so amazed that he took both birds home and sent one off to the taxidermist to have it mounted as a record of a most bizarre encounter.

Trigger happy

The North Yorkshire moors are home to much of the world's population of red grouse. The population is meticulously managed using centuries old techniques – including careful heather burning – to ensure that the species thrives and provides a sufficient surplus for shooting, a sport that brings much needed revenue into a remote part of England.

And that revenue can and does come from all over the world. Wealthy Guns from America, Australia and Europe arrive every August to shoot one of the most challenging game birds there is.

Those shooting grouse for the first time can find themselves in a tricky position. They may imagine that being a good shot is all that matters, but there is actually far more to driven grouse shooting than that. The real difficulty for many novices is understanding the rules. As the Guns are shooting parallel to each other there is a strict rule that no Gun shall shoot down the line (ie towards another Gun) but in the heat of the moment newcomers have been known to forget this most basic rule. Then there is the rule that you do not shoot every bird in sight – you do not poach your neighbour's birds. And again this is a tricky matter of judgment for the uninitiated.

But for at least one group of Guns from the Middle East the problem had more to do with basic shooting than basic etiquette. They were members of an oil rich family who spent much of the year living like playboys and travelling the world. Apart from driving expensive cars and staying in expensive hotels their one interest was shooting.

They had tried English driven pheasant shooting but were dazzled by what they heard about the difficulties and excitements of driven grouse shooting. Their aim wherever they went was to ensure success so when they planned their trip to the moors they bought the most modern and up to date weapons they could find – and they bought several each, together with an enormous quantity of ammunition.

But imagine the keeper's horror when he saw his guests climb down from their vehicles carrying a range of pump action shotguns and several semi automatic rifles.

The visitors were furious when the keeper explained to them through an interpreter that the purpose of the day was not to shoot as many birds as possible but to shoot well using the appropriate equipment. The Arabs insisted that as they had paid a lot of money to shoot they were entitled to shoot in any way they chose. The keeper quickly became aware that their attitude was likely to lead to all kinds of misdemeanours and uncontrolled shooting. After a tense stand-off during which the keeper resolutely refused to allow them to shoot, the police had to be called and the Arabs, despite their diplomatic status, were escorted off the moor.

5 Of Dogs and Men

Mobbed

A rough shooter who had spent decades pursuing hares and rabbits on the same coastal area of North Devon had experienced a number of unusual occurrences over the years – he'd been kicked by a rabbit, seen birds of prey fighting spectacularly in mid-air, watched a stoat dance till it had mesmerised a young rabbit but he had never been attacked while shooting.

He'd noticed a gradual increase in the number of gulls that flew back and forth to the nearest town where they collected scraps, but none had ever bothered him. Certainly some of the gulls – particularly the large herring gulls – had a reputation for aggressive behaviour but he had never had any trouble.

The trouble began when one sunny spring day he took a shot at a rabbit, bowled it over and then went to collect it. As he bent down he felt a thump on the back of his head. He was so startled that he slipped and fell. He instinctively reached behind to feel his head and neck and his hand came away soaked with blood. He stood up and had hardly had time to wonder what on earth was happening when out of the corner of his eye he saw something hurtling towards him.

Without thinking he ducked and then threw himself on the ground – just in time to hear the raucous angry cry of a gull that had missed his head by inches. The gull hovered and then began circling overhead, slowly gaining height and screeching continually.

He began running up the sloping field but was careful to glance behind now and then. It was lucky he did so for having gained sufficient height the gull had folded its wings and was hurtling towards him like a guided missile. Once again he was forced to throw himself to the ground but this time the gull raked his back – luckily his thick coat saved him from further injury.

He set off for home, bathed his wounds and thought no more about it. Gulls did occasionally attack humans and as humans increasingly encroached on their territory an attack now and then was inevitable.

A few weeks later he set off for an afternoon's shooting along the same piece of ground and no sooner had he arrived at the spot where he had been attacked than he noticed three gulls circling and crying out. He took no notice, carried on for roughly a quarter of a mile and then shot a pigeon as it took off noisily from a hedge. Hardly had he reached the bird when he heard the telltale sound of gulls. He could hardly believe it was going to happen again and it is easy to imagine his horror and alarm when he looked up and saw three gulls angrily heading towards him. Within seconds they had swooped and were angrily flying around and close to his head. It was only his decision to fire a shot that scared them off and prevent what might have been another bloody attack.

From that day on he always did his shooting a dozen miles away!

Hare today

Perhaps the most extraordinary coincidence ever recorded in the world of sporting shooting occurred at Capenoch in Scotland around 1900. A team of very grand Scottish aristocrats was shooting pheasants. Ground game was not allowed on this day but sport had been spectacular with high birds in a fierce wind.

During the early part of the afternoon a cock pheasant got up well ahead of the walking Guns and then cleverly used the wind to turn and soar back high over their heads. One man took a snap shot and the bird crumpled and fell.

As it tumbled towards the ground the Guns noticed a hare streaking across the open field and it is easy to imagine their astonishment when they saw the falling pheasant hit the running hare a decisive blow on the head. With more presence of mind they might have reached the stunned hare before it had time to recover its senses and stagger off like a drunk towards a distant hedgerow.

Crafty old bird

Until well into the twentieth century it was common practice in country districts to gather at harvest time to shoot. The Guns would stand around as the reaper went round each field gradually reducing the standing crop. At various stages – but particularly as the remaining area of crop began to disappear entirely – there would be a flurry of activity as rabbits, hares and various birds bolted past the waiting sportsmen.

A young chap still in his teens was shooting on this particular day. He had bagged a rabbit and a hare and was confident of further sport when suddenly a curious brown bird took off from the corn to his right. The boy fired and missed. But the bird seemed to only half-heartedly fly away so he ran after it and fired again.

The bird fell and the delighted boy picked it up and set off for home. Back at the house his mother put the bird, the rabbit and hare on the kitchen table. The boy stood by proudly watching these arrangements but then to his astonishment he thought he saw a slight twitch in the bird's eye. He shook his head in disbelief. But when it happened again he called out to his mother and the two stood staring at the immobile bird until his mother laughed and said that anyone watching would think they were mad. She got on with her work while the boy sat and started to clean his gun. At that very moment, the bird leapt to its feet, jumped from the table and ran through the open door into the garden at high speed with the young man and his mother in hot pursuit. But it was too late – once in the open air the crafty bird took to its wings and sailed off rapidly into the distance.

Sniping

After a fairly hopeless day shooting along the banks of Norfolk's River Ouse, two Edwardian sportsmen finally put up a snipe on a very muddy part of the foreshore. They had no dog – it was ill at home – and the snipe fell well out towards the river. Regretfully they decided it wasn't worth the risk of trying to retrieve the bird so they left it and headed for home.

They still had more than a mile to walk before reaching their cottage and by this time the wind was blowing fiercely which slowed them down. Nearly half an hour later they reached the cottage door and found the wife of one of the two sportsmen standing in the drive, together with their daughter. The two women were examining a dead snipe.

They explained that just a few minutes earlier they'd been sitting in the garden to the side of the drive when they heard a wild scrabbling in the trees above their heads. A moment later and the snipe – now dead – dropped almost at their feet. The two men examined the bird and noticed the mud on its breast and under its wings – unmistakably mud from the river.

The two men immediately thought this must be the bird they had shot and left back on the river mud more than a mile away. It seemed too incredible to be true.

The only way to be sure was to retrace their steps to the river but this time with a dog. This they did but despite sending the dog out all along the area where they thought the bird had fallen there was no sign of it. The bird in the drive must have been the same bird they'd shot by the river. It had obviously recovered sufficiently to overtake the two men on their way home, before dropping dead just ten feet from their front door.

Gun tongue

Victorian newspapers loved bizarre stories and since sport at that time meant shooting and fishing rather than football and tennis they loved reporting strange stories from the shooting field. The *Durham Advertiser* for 1865 records a particularly odd story from what was then a remote part of the country.

Out one bitterly cold January day on the moors near Sedgefield a young man and his friend had been shooting throughout the long day, but it had been one of those days when nothing goes right. They'd had plenty of shots, but hadn't bagged a thing. Every shot was wide and they were near the end of the day with nothing to show for their efforts. Much of the problem probably lay in the intense cold – neither man could remember a day so cold and it was probably affecting their reactions and judgement of range and distance.

Before giving up and heading for home they decided to have one last try for a snipe over a nearby bog. By this time the temperature had dropped even further, but as they reached the end of the marshy ground a bird got up and one of the young men put up his gun and tried for it. The shot fell wide. Then thunderstruck, the young man found he could not remove his hand from the barrel of the gun. The trigger hand that had been on the stock was fine but where the barrels of the gun had rested on the palm of his left hand the gun had stuck fast. The frost was so intense that his wet hand had stuck instantly and immovably to the steel. When they tried to prise gun and hand apart the skin from the man's hand began to peel away and the blood that flowed instantly froze making the situation even worse.

Wondering what on earth he could do the young man had an idea. He would put his mouth down near where his hand was stuck and breathe gently to warm gunmetal and hand up sufficiently for the two to be parted. How it happened no one was afterwards able to remember but in trying to breathe on his hand the young man actually managed to touch the gun barrel just ahead of the glued hand with his tongue. This too instantly stuck immovably. The young man was in a desperate plight with his hand and face attached firmly to the front half of his gun and no prospect of releasing either. It must also have been an incredibly awkward and painful position to maintain as the light failed and the temperature dropped even further.

Relief came only after a half-mile walk to the nearest farmhouse. Here a kettle of warm water solved a painful problem, but both hand and tongue had lost a great deal of skin as a result.

Ghost bunny

A crofter in a remote part of the Scottish Highlands regularly walked twenty or more miles in a day in search of sport and was happy to return with a few birds or a couple of rabbits, but an incident occurred one stormy winter's day that changed his shooting forever.

He had walked miles along the sea edge without seeing anything worth shooting when a rabbit suddenly bolted from a tussock right under his nose. He counted to three and fired. The rabbit tumbled over perhaps twenty yards ahead of him and he shouldered his gun and walked ahead to pick it up. When he reached the spot where he had shot it there was no sign of a rabbit anywhere. He assumed it must have tumbled into a hole and thought no more about it. A week later exactly the same thing happened, but this time as soon as he realised he could not find the rabbit he noticed a thick sea mist rolling towards him.

Within seconds he was completely lost, despite knowing every inch of the ground for miles around. It was with the utmost difficulty that he got back to his cottage. Curiously on both occasions he had been shooting within a few hundred yards of the remains of a Second World War fighter plane that had crashed during the war and been left to rot where it fell.

When he was next shooting in the area he went over to the remains of the wreck and was astonished at how much of it remained intact. There was a great deal of rust but the pilot's leather seat was still there and on the ground nearby the tattered remains of a boot and other scraps of clothing.

By this time it was growing dark so he turned to set off for home. He'd gone only a few hundred yards when he heard the deep drone of an aircraft. It sounded horribly low and very close by. A moment later and straight ahead he saw a plane coming towards him just a hundred or so feet above the ground. It was clearly in trouble and passed over his head with a terrifying roar before disappearing over the rising ground behind him. For a moment that seemed to last forever there was silence and then a huge explosion. He raced up the incline and, reaching the summit just a minute or two after he'd heard the explosion, looked down the valley before him expecting to see the burning wreck of an aeroplane. But there was nothing. Only the sound of the wind and evening coming on. He was convinced he must have imagined the whole thing, perhaps after spending too long around the melancholy ruins of that old aircraft, but despite dismissing the incident from his mind he was careful never again to visit that area either to shoot or to walk.

6 High Birds and Hedge-Hoppers

Jewel thief

The pleasures of shooting have always had more to do with being out in the fields and woods than with the simple mechanics of firing a gun. The old adage that one is never so close to nature than when in pursuit of it reflects a deep truth about all country sports. But to this pleasure must always be added the pleasure of bringing something home for the pot. One young man out with dog and gun in the Surrey woods in the 1930s found that he was able to bring something home for the pot and for the police!

He'd had a successful day and had stopped for lunch with several pigeons and a pheasant already in his bag. He had promised the keeper that if he could remove a few grey squirrels he would. They had caused great damage to many of the young trees in the wood and their numbers were getting out of hand.

Within an hour of finishing lunch he had shot several squirrels and blasted a number of their drays or nests out of the trees. Almost the last shot of the day brought a large dray down and as it fell the young man saw something glinting among the debris. He rummaged through the fallen leaves and sticks and found a heavy gold bracelet.

Magpies commonly steal brightly coloured objects and incorporate them in their nests but there is no evidence that squirrels have similar habits. Perhaps the young man's shot had knocked down a hidden magpie's nest or perhaps the bracelet had been hidden in the tree by a thief who planned to return at some time in the future to collect it.

Whichever way he looked at it the young man was baffled and his astonishment was all the greater when he had the bracelet valued and was told that it was made from 22 carat gold – exceptionally pure and very valuable. He took the bracelet to the police who advertised in local newspapers to find its owner, but no one ever came forward and it was eventually returned to the young man who had found it. He was so delighted that he sold it and promptly bought a new gun!

World's most exclusive club?

To join the little known, but remarkably exclusive, Woodcock Club you must shoot a right and left at woodcock. It's no good shooting one woodcock, waiting thirty seconds or a minute and then shooting another. Both birds must be in the air at the same time and you must get one with the first barrel and the other with the second.

Woodcock are solitary birds that fly erratically so a right and left is no easy task – which is why the club has only a relatively small number of members.

One man who didn't join managed to shoot a right and left at woodcock without even being aware he'd done it. He was out in a Devon in the 1890s enjoying a bit of rough shooting through the local woods which were hardly ever shot for Devon in those days was still remote and difficult to get to.

The sportsman reached a ride and spotted a rabbit crossing to the right. He took a pot shot and missed but at that very moment another rabbit crossed to the left and without thinking the young man fired his second barrel at it but missed again.

Cursing his luck he checked at the edge of the ride just in case he had in fact hit one or other rabbit and discovered to his astonishment two woodcock about three yards apart but in the exact line along which he had fired.

Gun gone

Guns are important to those who shoot. It is not just that a gun is a practical piece of equipment without which the sport would be impossible. No. For some a gun is rather like a good friend. For others it is a work of art, which explains why so many people buy guns that have been beautifully engraved or that have beautifully figured stocks. So, when a gun is lost or damaged, it is a serious matter. And one of the strangest stories from the late nineteenth century concerns the disappearance of a particularly magnificent example of the gunmaker's art.

The gun – a beautiful Purdey – was owned by a wealthy Northumberland farmer who set off every Saturday in the season to shoot whatever game came along. He enjoyed his day more for the walk with his dogs than for the quality of the shooting, which was only average at best.

On this particular January day he had stopped for lunch at a place he knew well. It gave wonderful views out across the Tyne Valley and was his regular stopping place. He ate his sandwiches, had a few sips from his hip flask and enjoyed the view of wild moorland and distant blue sky. A few hundred yards below the mossy bank on which he sat was a small stream that had been his favourite trout beck as a child. On a whim he decided to go down and see if he could spot a few trout. The stream was high after recent rain but he wandered up and down for a while without seeing any sign of a fish. At last he returned to the bank where he had had his lunch. He prepared to set off and reached out for his gun. It had vanished. He searched all around the bank and wandered back along the way he always came. He searched behind nearby rocks and retraced his steps down to the stream. He was absolutely baffled. He hadn't seen anyone all morning so it was impossible that someone could have stolen the gun. He became ever more panic stricken and hurried back and forth across the rough tussocky grass moving further and further away from the place where he was sure he must have left the gun. All afternoon he searched but with no luck and as the light began to fade he conceded defeat and headed for home.

He returned the following day and searched again but this time with his son. The gun had it seemed vanished into thin air.

Months later he was out shooting once again and he returned to the bank where he had lost his gun. By now he had reconciled himself to the loss and hardly gave it a thought. He ate his lunch, but with his gun – an old Westley Richards this time – laid across his knees rather than propped up on the bank, just to be on the safe side. He finished his sandwiches, smoked his pipe and got ready to set off. He called up the dogs, checked his bag and was about to leave when, on the ground not six feet away, he saw the Purdey he had lost six months earlier. He was so astonished that he could hardly think. The gun was just as he had left it – if it had been out in all weathers for six months it would have been covered with rust, but it seemed to have barely a mark on it.

He set off for home immediately, delighted with his good fortune. For the next twenty years until his death he wondered every day what had happened to his gun for those six months. He never found out.

The bets are on!

Until the coming of the railway and in many areas for long after its arrival, country people had to look locally for their entertainment. Shooting and fishing were always popular and poorer people could perhaps at best afford a bit of pigeon or rabbit shooting but that didn't mean they couldn't enjoy grand shoots in a slightly different way. At large estates near big urban centres – particularly places such as Welbeck in Nottinghamshire – a tradition grew up in which working men, miners and factory workers watched the formal driven shoots from a trackway, footpath or even from the road.

In County Durham miners not only watched the grand estate shoots but they bet on which Gun would hit what. Apparently many grandees complained about the rows of spectators who watched their every move, but if they were on the public highway nothing could be done and shooting, for the first and perhaps only time on its history, became something of a popular spectator sport.

At Welbeck the spectators even began to shout encouragement at their favourite Guns while a poor showing among the Guns would be met with howls of disapproval and derogatory comments.

Large sums of money were often won and lost on various bets and it must have felt rather odd to be an aristocrat providing entertainment for the working classes.

The eyes have it

Back in the 1970s and 1980s, the clay shooting circuit in England was big enough to support hundreds if not thousands of Guns who trekked round the country each weekend attending as many events as possible. The best Shots on the circuit could make a very decent living from the numerous prizes on offer – in a single weekend a good Gun might win cash, a television, a car and an exotic holiday.

One well-known Shot on the circuit made his name not for his prowess in hitting clays but for his singular ability never to win anything. Despite his failure ever to win a prize he attended most of the major competitions and many of the smaller ones. But the other Guns loved him – he was funny, always relaxed and ready to share a joke and he had one quite remarkable ability – he almost always hit every bird thrown from the highest towers. Since these were by far the most difficult shots the other Guns were astonished. High tower clays might be anything from 120-140 feet above ground and few of the other Guns ever managed to hit more than one or two of the ten high birds required.

Why could he hit the really difficult birds but not the relatively easy ones? The mystery was solved when he announced one sunny Saturday that he had been to his optician and been told that he had developed an eye defect that gave him a huge advantage on distant clays and a huge disadvantage on closer, faster moving clays. On the high birds his eye problems was making him shoot well ahead of the target – but that was precisely what was needed to allow for the time it took for the shot to reach such exceptionally high birds.

The bemused clay shooter had a pair of glasses made to compensate for his eye problem and he started to hit far more of the standard birds – the crossers, going-away clays and so on – but he always took the glasses off for those high birds! His fellow Guns joked that this must be a unique instance where a disability gave him a huge advantage!

Hope springs eternal

The great Victorian eccentric Lord Francis Hope accidentally shot himself in the foot at a pheasant drive. He carried on shooting while standing on one leg and the foot was later amputated. Bizarrely, Hope's brother, the Duke of Newcastle, had also shot himself in the foot a few years earlier. He too had carried on shooting until the end of the drive and he too had his foot amputated. Both men claimed they would simply learn to hop, which is what they did.

A bad year for life and limb

On English pheasant shoots the year 1848 seems to have been a bad one, but the accidents of that year reveal as nothing else the extraordinary stiff upper lip mentality of earlier aristocratic generations.

When a beater lost an eye in a bramble bush one of the Guns

expressed his sympathies for the man. Immediately another said: 'Oh, you'll make him soft. He doesn't care about his eye.' In the same year the Duke of Gloucester, a famously haphazard shot, blinded his equerry in one eye, and then complained that the man made 'such a fuss about it'.

Also in 1848, a man shooting in Norfolk shot and killed – by accident of course – a boy who was beating. Asked if he wasn't terribly upset by the death he said: 'I was lucky it was a boy and his mother was prepared to accept £5 for the inconvenience.'

Hare-raising

In the early nineteenth century at Lord Coke's great house at Holkham, in Norfolk, a well-known but rather eccentric old professor was invited to shoot. He had never held a gun before so was placed at the corner of the covert. Later, Lord Coke asked him: 'Well, what sport? You have been firing pretty often.'

'Hsssh!' said the professor, 'there it goes again', and he was just raising his gun to his shoulder when a man walked quietly out from the bushes. It was one of the beaters who had been placed there as a stop, and his leather gaiters, seen dimly through the bushes, had been mistaken for a hare by the professor.

He had been firing at 'it' whenever he saw it move, and had been surprised by its tenacity of life. More surprising was the fact that the man had never discovered that the professor was shooting at him!

Making a splash

Two rough shooters out for a day in the Scottish Highlands in the 1930s had failed to shoot a single thing despite walking for most of the day and trying places where they had been successful on many previous occasions.

They were nervous about returning home to their wives empty handed but by now the light was fading and they had all but run out of ideas. They stopped by a small fast flowing stream and ate the last of their sandwiches. Neither spoke and they simply stared gloomily ahead across the water. Then in an instant both men saw the answer: a salmon had thrown itself up the small waterfall that crashed down between two rocks a little upstream of where they sat. They loaded their guns and waited for the next fish. Ten minutes later there was a splash, a fish threw itself out of the water and was promptly brought down by one of the Guns. It drifted to within a few feet of the shore and all the men had to do was stoop and lift it out of the water. The next fish to show itself suffered the same fate and the men, not wishing to push their luck, immediately packed up and set off for home, where they were promptly arrested for poaching! The local river keeper had watched the whole thing and alerted the police.

7 Tales from a Foreign Field

Afghan antics

Long before Afghanistan descended into its most recent bout of madness it was a country where ancient sophisticated civilisations had thrived – the Buddhists of Bamiyan for example, whose famous rock-carvings were destroyed by the Taliban. But other less well-known cultures linked to neighbouring Iran and India built extraordinary mosques and monuments the ruins of which still survive.

Ancient Afghans loved sport of every kind – from falconry to coursing – but by the mid twentieth century much of the country's abundant game had been pointlessly destroyed. The arrival of machine guns and automatic rifles simply led to game of every species being shot on sight for no good reason.

Dove shooting had been popular and this more restrained sport had been a particular enthusiasm of the ruling elite and only rarely attracting the insanely trigger happy. But on one occasion in the 1950s a group of tribesmen got together for what must be one of the most bizarre dove shoots in history.

An American reporter described what happened. Having arrived in the small village where he was staying, twenty local men embraced each other and exchanged polite greetings before sitting down cross-legged in a circle. Apart from an occasional cough and a great deal of spitting no one spoke and no one moved for the next two hours!

Then for no apparent reason the most senior man in the group went into a nearby mud hut. A few minutes later the others all trailed into the hut and again sat in a circle cradling their rifles and machine guns. They ate lunch and then after a further silent hour of sitting they trailed outside again.

A few boys appeared carrying half-a-dozen roughly made wooden crates. Each crate contained perhaps a dozen scrawny looking rock doves. The men lined up. The boys placed the crates on the ground and then withdrew about a hundred yards either side. Each boy held a length of string that ran across the sand to one of the crates. The men stood perhaps sixty yards away facing the crates. At a signal the boys began shouting loudly and tugging on their string. Several of the wooden crates collapsed releasing their birds in a noisy flurry of wings. One or two only half collapsed and the birds slipped gradually away. While this was happening the men fired wildly in the direction of the birds. Most fired from the hip completely inaccurately but the noise was deafening. After about a minute the shooting stopped as suddenly as it had begun and the men trooped off back into the mud hut. Not a single bird had been hit. The boys ran off.

The American asked his guide what on earth was going on. The guide replied: 'The headman knows about driven English shooting and tries to persuade his family that it will have a civilising influence on them and that if they participate regularly Western Aid agencies will pay money to set up driven shoots here in Afghanistan. Whenever they have a visitor, particularly an American or someone from Britain, they want to show that they know how to organise such things.'

Never mind the beaters

Shooting (particularly if it was really easy) was a favourite pastime of the Russian tsars and of their successors in the Communist ruling party. Having ousted the Russian Royal family, a long series of communist rulers took quickly and easily to the pleasures and pursuits of the people they'd got rid of.

President Leonid Brezhnev was far too nervous to risk hunting big animals such as wolf and bear so he had them captured and tied to a tree before shooting them and latterly he did this from his wheelchair. Like Russian hotels, transport and manufacturing, Russian sporting shooting was bizarrely organised and the Russian obsession was entirely with showing the rest of the world that everything in Russia was bigger and better than anything similar to be found elsewhere.

Numerous journalists and diplomats from the West were often invited to enjoy a day's shooting during their time in Russia and all those who wrote about the experience were astonished at the cavalier attitude to safety and animal welfare.

One journalist who visited several shoots in Russia during the late 1960s and early 1970s remarked on the chaos of the organisation, the lack of safety rules and the obsession with big bags. It was as if, he later reported, those on the shoot felt they would be sent to the Gulag if they failed to shoot a new world record number of birds.

Senior Politburo members were particularly aggressive in their pursuit of maximum bags and there was little in the way of conversation between drives – the whole thing was taken incredibly seriously.

Immature birds were shot continually, along with birds flying so low that they could have been knocked down with a stick. One journalist asked several Guns if they did not think it rather unsporting to shoot low birds but these enquiries were met with blank looks of incomprehension. And many difficult high birds were left unsaluted – the Guns it seems didn't shoot at difficult birds because they didn't want to waste cartridges!

On one notorious shoot, as the birds began to come over an English journalist dived for cover – the Russian Guns were so befuddled that they were firing along the line, in other words towards each other!

Lead shot was flying everywhere so the journalist decided his best bet was to keep his head down – in fact he lay on the ground and simply pretended he was tired while the fusillade went on above his head. The next drive saw several of the Guns disappearing into the woods with a number of glamorous young women who seemed to have appeared out of thin air and then, on the final drive, came the most remarkable incident of all.

The birds were already flying over and the Guns were blazing in the now familiar fashion but the journalist was worried as he had already caught a glimpse now and then of the beaters gradually approaching. He decided to stop shooting.

Immediately the Gun next to him along the line shouted.

'Why have you stopped shooting?'

'The beaters are too close,' said the journalist.

'But they are not armed!' came the reply.

Taking an elephant apart

Today the adventurous young try to swim the English Channel, sail round the world or walk across Afghanistan, but in Victorian England the great adventurers were often big game hunters. These were men who risked their lives in pursuit of savage animals such as lion and tiger and the tales of their exploits became the stuff of schoolboy stories. The idea that too much shooting would lead to the extinction of a species never seems to have occurred to anyone, but then the world seemed a much bigger place a century and more ago than it does now. One of the best known of Victorian hunter-sportsmen was Roualeyn Cumming. Now almost entirely forgotten, he travelled across Africa with a large band of local men employed to carry his vast quantity of European necessities. His men were fed on the game that Cumming shot as they marched along.

Later in life he wrote about his experiences in Africa and he recalled one quite remarkable incident he witnessed after shooting a large bull elephant.

No sooner had the elephant been shot than dozens of Cumming's bearers surrounded the carcase and began cutting away large sections of skin from the side of the elephant that lay uppermost. Beneath that first thick outer layer there were several inner coats of skin, which were removed with great delicacy and later made into highly efficient water carriers. The flesh of the elephant was then cut in huge chunks from the ribs before each individual rib was carefully removed. Cumming was impressed by the precision cutting carried out by his men but that was as nothing compared to their work on the elephant's intestines.

For the local men this was where the really nourishing meat and fat was to be found but to get it the men – half a dozen of them – had to climb into the elephant's inside where they disappeared from view into the mass of guts.

Hands appeared now and then from inside the bloody mess handing out chunks of fat and, while this went on, frantic activity round all other parts of the carcase gradually whittled it down to bare bone.

As they worked all the villagers smeared every inch of their bodies from the crown of the head to the sole of the foot with the contents of the elephant's gut as well as blood and other gore. The men were so keen on this that one man would help another by spreading the slimy bloody mess on the other's back. Throughout the entire proceeding there was a deafening babble of voices as the men wrestled and elbowed their way frantically in and out of the carcase. Cumming never forgot how the massive animal was so skilfully taken apart and he later wrote that he was astonished how almost nothing was wasted.

Taking a tiger

No book of shooting stories would be complete without something from one of the greatest of all big game hunter, Jim Corbett. Corbett became well known through his books on shoots and life in general in India in the early years of the twentieth century. He was also a remarkably prescient man who, long before it was fashionable, wrote about the dangers of over-exploiting nature. He was famous for hunting man-eating tigers, which were occasionally a serious problem in rural India, but he knew that it would be relatively easy for man to make the Indian population of tigers extinct. He urged restraint at a time when restraint was simply not the fashion.

But Corbett also loved sporting shooting and he was a practical man

who regularly shot birds sitting if that was a more certain way to ensure he didn't miss lunch.

He spent much of his life in India and though his work retains the predominant view of the nineteenth century Englishman – that the natives, as they were called, are somehow inherently inferior – he was, in other respects, a remarkably humane man. He also wrote some of the most exciting accounts ever written of shooting in remote parts of the world. One of his most astonishing stories concerns the events at the end of a long day shooting pheasants and jungle fowl in the foothills of the Himalayas. He had only a mile or so to go before reaching home when he was caught in a storm, but this was no ordinary storm. It followed a lengthy drought and was quite terrifying. Corbett describes hailstones as big as eggs smashing into plants and trees and knocking birds of every description out of the sky. Crops were flattened and birds as big as vultures lay strewn across a broad swathe of land.

Corbett would have been badly injured if he had not reached cover quickly and he heard later that it was not uncommon for cattle, monkeys and even children to be killed by these hailstone storms.

Corbett was no stranger to extraordinary events and it was on a shooting expedition soon after the hailstone storm that he came across something equally remarkable. A buffalo had gone berserk in his local village causing a huge and damaging stampede of all the other buffalo in the herd. The villagers had eventually managed to shoot the maddened animal, but Corbett wanted to investigate the incident. He examined the dead animal and discovered that huge chunks of flesh had been torn from its back. There was no obvious explanation for this, so Corbett laid baits for the culprit. A few nights later from his treetop hiding place he saw a poorly nourished tiger attack the bait, but the tiger used only its claws to rip at the meat and Corbett saw that in some accident it had lost most of its lower jaw. Unable to use its jaws to throttle the buffalo in the normal way it had obviously leapt on to its back and begun eating the poor animal even as it ran off. Understandably the buffalo had panicked and in its panic stricken charge it had caused a stampede of the whole herd.

Wrestling, pursued by bear

G.S.Wodeman was a British Civil Servant stationed in Sri Lanka (or Ceylon as it was formerly known), just after the Great War. One of his great friends – and his regular shooting companion – was a Mr Festing. One of Wodeman's duties was to check regularly on the state of the local villages. He did this by simply walking through them every week usually with his friend Festing.

One hot day towards the end of August 1921 Wodeman was making his way along his usual route accompanied by Festing who carried his favourite shotgun and hoped they might shoot a jungle cock for breakfast. Half-a-dozen local villagers followed behind. Festing gradually wandered ahead of Wodeman. Then something went terribly wrong.

The path made a sharp right turn. Wodeman saw Festing go rigid as he turned the corner. Festing put his gun up to his shoulder. The villagers vanished.

Two very angry bears were charging down towards Festing who immediately fired both barrels.

One bear ran off to the side of the path and into the jungle. The other hurled itself at Festing and knocked him down. The two rolled on the ground with Festing swearing at the top of his voice and thrashing his arms and legs, the bear roaring continually. Wodeman ran over to the two and seizing the gun, which had fallen on the ground, he began belting the bear round the head with it until the stock broke. He couldn't reload and fire as all the cartridges were in Festing's pocket.

The bear turned its attention to Wodeman who was badly mauled and might have been killed but for Festing who used the shotgun barrels to attack the bear again.

Finally the bear released Wodeman and the two men were able to run back towards the village. The bear retreated into the jungle.

As suddenly as they'd vanished the villagers reappeared. When they took stock of the situation the two men found they were really quite badly injured. Wodeman's arm had been bitten through to the bone and Festing's thigh was torn in several places and his face was a mass of cuts and bruises. But they were lucky to have escaped with their lives.

Ibex in Nepal

Remote and dangerous, Nepal held an enduring fascination for Victorian big game hunters. And the creature they sought above all others was the ibex, a beautiful and now rare member of the goat family. Apart from the sheer difficulty of getting close enough to these extremely elusive creatures for a shot, the attraction was the ibex's superb curving horns.

One of the most fearless ibex hunters of the nineteenth century, Major Neville Taylor, was perhaps also one of the maddest. He trekked across much of the Himalayas in a career that lasted more than thirty years. He shot some spectacular ibex but also saw killed numerous trackers and sherpas who accompanied his various expeditions.

He was an expert shot but like most sportsmen he had his off days. On at least one occasion he missed three ibex within the space of three hours. The final straw came when he fired at a fourth ibex only to see it disappear over a snowy ridge. He was cursing his fate when his guide, a Pashtu called Lassoo, insisted that the ibex was almost certainly dead. Neville, despite his experience, was astonished at this and insisted that he'd missed the shot. But Neville also knew enough to know that if Lassoo insisted then Lassoo was probably right. They walked to the edge of the crest and there a few hundred feet below was the fallen ibex. They were faced with a huge problem because the superb beast (with superb horns) was gradually slipping towards a ravine. As they watched it reached the cliff edge and vanished. Neville was distraught at the loss of a particularly fine pair of horns but Lassoo offered to creep to the edge of the ravine to see if the beast could still be recovered. It was an extremely dangerous manoeuvre and both men – Neville insisted on accompanying his guide – could easily have been killed.

The ibex had fallen 200 feet and had become wedged on a rocky outcrop with its head hanging over the edge and the horns undamaged. Lassoo immediately offered to climb down the treacherous slope. Neville, despite all his adventures, was astonished and always said he had never seen anything as brave in his life.

Lassoo seemed to grip the icy cliff face with the ends of his fingertips Neville later reported. 'I would not have gone with him for the world,' the major said. 'It was only what I saw this day that made me realise what a hill man can do and that no European could ever hope to attain their skill in the most inhospitable conditions.'

Perched on the tiny ledge the guide was able to cut the horns from the ibex's head and climb back up the sheer face of the ravine where an astonished Neville congratulated him on his remarkable climb.

Last minute shot

William Cotton Oswell, a great friend of explorer David Livingstone, was a hero to thousands of Victorian schoolboys who read avidly his stories of big game hunting in Africa.

Oswell was nothing if not conservative, which may explain why he insisted on always using the same 10 bore muzzle-loading Purdey despite its increasingly dilapidated appearance. Battered by endless encounters with rocks and trees, rhino and elephants it looked like a length of old rusty pipe.

And if Oswell's gun was strange then his technique was even stranger. He rode his favourite pony furiously toward any herd of animals in which he'd taken an interest and once within range he'd leap from the animal's back, kneel down and fire all in one smooth movement honed by years of practice. For deer of various kinds this was all well and good but with rhino, buffalo and elephant it was far riskier because Oswell always waited until the animal had begun its charge before firing and he often waited until the beast was within just twenty or thirty feet thus leaving no margin at all for error. One misfire and he was dead.

Rhino and elephant often charged him as he leaped from his horse, but there is no record of his ever making a run for it. Instead he would crouch and fire and despite the sorry state of his old rifle it never jammed or misfired. If it had he would certainly have been killed. Oswell claimed that the reason he hardly ever wounded an animal was precisely because he made sure he shot them at point blank range. Very few other big game hunters adopted this technique and those who were foolhardy enough to try it did not usually survive long. It was probably Oswell's absolute confidence in his abilities that saved him: 'If you are afraid of dying, don't try it,' he once observed.

Oswell would have been astonished at the idea that Africa's wildlife could possibly be damaged by sporting shooting and he never lost his enthusiasm for the wildlife of the Continent. In one of his books he movingly describes seeing springbok herds so vast it took half a day for them to pass.

Oswell always insisted that buffalo were the most dangerous of all African animals – far more so than elephant or even lion. An angry buffalo was a very difficult animal to kill. Oswell and other hunters reported hitting buffalo a dozen times only to see the animal shake its head and charge again.

Only once did Oswell break the habit of a lifetime and try shooting at a buffalo from a horseback position. Having taken his shot he saw the buffalo fall and immediately rode up to it. No sooner had he passed the dead animal than he heard a strange noise and glancing back saw the buffalo leap to its feet and begin its charge. Oswell dug in his spurs to try to escape the enraged animal but it was too late – his horse was gored and he himself thrown to the ground where he lay unconscious for a few moments. When he came to his senses he found his horse nearby with its stomach torn out. There was no trace of the buffalo and no sign of its blood. For the rest of his life Oswell believed that the buffalo had tricked him, but he never again shot a large animal from horseback.

Lion tamer

The great thing about the British Empire was that it gave the servants of the Empire – the thousands of civil servants from Britain who settled in India and Africa to administer the empire – the chance to shoot and fish in entirely unspoiled areas.

From pheasants and rabbits in England the sportsman soon graduated to buffalo and elephant and it many ways it was their tales of encounters with these dangerous animals – published in seemingly endless books during the latter nineteenth century – that fuelled the English schoolboy's love of adventure.

One of these long forgotten writers described a scene he witnessed in an African village that put all his own adventures into the shade. The writer had been shooting wildfowl on a remote lake and on the return journey stopped at a small village for water. He watched a group of women working in a field at the edge of the village and then noticed that from a nearby clearing a young man was calling to them.

A moment later and to the utter astonishment of the Englishman, a young lion suddenly appeared in the clearing, knocked the young man down and began dragging him towards the nearby undergrowth.

While he watched and long before he had time himself to react in any way, the Englishman saw a young woman run quietly after the lion and, to Oswell's never-ceasing astonishment, she grabbed it by the tail with both hands, dug her heels into the sand and simply hung on. The lion had to slow down.

Hampered by the man in its mouth and the woman dragging behind it, the lion stopped. Immediately the woman let go of the tail, ran a few steps forward and jumped on the lion's back. She then whacked it back and forth across the head and shoulders with her short, heavy-handed hoe. Almost immediately the lion dropped the young man and slunk away. The young man finding himself released brushed himself down and began talking quite calmly to his rescuer. The two then wandered off back towards the centre of the village.

Man eater

The great legends of shooting in India during the Raj invariably involved man-eating tigers.

One man-eater on the Manipur Border of India and Burma became extraordinarily well known simply because it survived so long on a diet of villagers and domestic buffalo. Everything was tried against this particular rogue – stake-outs using tethered goats and chunks of buffalo, but the tiger was too wily and invariably failed to appear while the marksmen were in position.

The tiger led a charmed life and was regularly seen sizing up policemen on their rounds and children on the way to school. He had often attacked hunters and villagers but was careful to avoid groups of men. The man-eater of Tammu, as this tiger was known, only once threw caution to the winds and to the astonishment of all pursued a party of four heavily armed hunters down a tributary of the Chindwin River.

The men were travelling by canoe when they spotted a tiger moving quickly through the dense jungle on the side of the river nearest the boat. They could tell that this was not an accidental sighting because the tiger remained in view as they continued their journey. Eerily it seemed to keep pace with their boat. As they reached a broad glide in the river and their pace slackened they saw the tiger leap into the water and swim towards them

Only by rowing vigorously did they begin to leave the tiger behind – it had reached to within a few yards of the back of the boat before it changed its mind and headed back to the bank. Back on the bank it continued to keep abreast of the boat, but bizarrely, after that encounter, the man-eater was never seen again.

Trigger-happy churchman

The Abbot of Tepl owned and managed vast acres around the town of Marienbad in Germany and he was keen to attract English sportsmen to his shoot. Such was the fame of his shoot he thought he would start by inviting Edward VII. The king, an enthusiastic shot, set out for Marienbad, lured as much as anything by the extraordinary lunches that were a feature of the estate.

When the day of the king's shoot arrived the abbot decided to leave nothing to chance so he had thousands of extra birds brought in by train in hundreds of specially built cages to augment the birds already on the ground.

On arrival Edward was delighted to discover that lunch began shortly after the completion of the first drive – it started early for the simple reason that it had to in order to allow enough time for the guests to work their way through the vast pile of food spread out before the guests. It was altogether a very special group of Guns for the king had been joined by several dukes and earls as well as a dozen or so distinguished monks who were friends of the abbot and hundreds of spectators, eager to see the king of England.

Those monks who were of the shooting party wielded ancient guns of every description to take part in the shoot and the scene as lunch ended and the second drive began, was described by one observer as astonishingly chaotic.

By the time the shoot resumed most of the Guns including the king were drunk or very drunk, but they were helped to their butts and the first drive of the afternoon began. Then in some vague, perhaps almost instinctive way, the great swarms of beaters moved off like birds on migration and the fun – in theory at least – began.

Ahead of the king's butt were two small boys with kites high above them. The idea of the kites was to funnel the partridges above the king to ensure he had most of the sport, but bad planning and placing the kite boys too close together meant that most of the partridges ran past the king rather than take to the air. The vast numbers of partridges began to get caught up among the crowds of spectators, but despite what was rapidly turning into a farce – and despite the fact that the Guns later reported hardly firing a shot – the abbot declared the total bag for the day to be almost one hundred head. The truth was that that this low but respectable figure had been achieved by counting all the partridges that had died in the train, flown into trees or were caught by the dogs.

Tongue lashing

With British sportsmen shooting in various parts of the Empire it was inevitable that reports would filter back to England now and then of bizarre incidents and extraordinary days in the field. Few however were stranger than the story concerning a local who tried to shoot a buffalo in South Africa.

The old man had set out from his village with an old flintlock gun and was never seen alive again. Trackers later pieced together what had probably happened to him. From the evidence of hoof print it seems that the old man had spotted a group of buffalo – probably quite a small group or he would not have risked tackling them alone – and had spent the day tracking them. He clearly decided in the end to try a shot but merely wounded the animal, which then charged at him. The old man made a run for it and managed to reach a big projecting rock.

What followed was an example of the kind of behaviour that made the buffalo more feared in Africa than either the rhino or the elephant. First it tried to gore the hunter by pushing its head under the rock but the gap was too narrow. The hunter had only just been able to get under the rock and only by lying lengthways. A patch of the hunter's thigh was very close to the edge of the rock and though the buffalo couldn't reach it with his horns he could reach it with his tongue.

He began licking the bare patch of flesh and he licked it with his massive sandpaper textured tongue until it began to bleed. He licked on after the blood started to run and continued until most of the muscle lay bare and the blood flowed profusely. The hunter could do nothing. As the buffalo would not go away he could not come out from under his rock and he couldn't escape the buffalo's tongue. When they found him his leg had been licked almost to the bone and he had bled to death.

One can only hope that the hunter lost consciousness soon after the blood began to flow and death would probably have come quickly after that.

Princely shots

Friends from childhood, Prince Hohenloe and Baron Veitinghoff had shot together hundreds of times over the years. All their outings had gone well until one fateful day towards the end of the nineteenth century, when, in a seemingly impenetrable Austrian wood they decided to try to call up a few stags using an artificial caller. They separated, agreeing to meet later for lunch.

The day wore on. The two men wandered and lost track of each other and of time. As darkness fell they had no idea where they were and unwittingly had wandered within a few hundred yards of each other. They were both still occasionally using their calls and being now so close each heard the other's call, thought it was a real stag and believed he was about to get a shot.

The undergrowth was so thick that neither man could see much, particularly as the light was beginning to fade. At last, fed up with his failure to catch even a glimpse of the presumed stag, the prince fired three times at what he thought was the slight tinge of a beast glimpsed between the trees. The first bullet ricocheted off the baron's cartridge belt; the second hit his solid gold watch and the third buried itself deeply but harmlessly in a pocket book stuffed thick with papers. By a miracle the baron was unharmed if shaken and he was still recovering from his shock when the prince appeared with a look of utter astonishment on his face.

Portuguese man of war

In shooting, manners – or more precisely good manners – matter perhaps even more than skill. The British traditionally (according at least to the British) have very good shooting manners where foreigners are less reliable in this respect. This led to some very awkward moments in those great Edwardian days when foreign heads of state were invited to England. They were far too grand to be told what to do but had to be kept under some control if beaters and dogs were not to be shot. The problem was particularly acute on aristocratic estates where the owners were frequently related to German or Russian families.

Lady Cardigan recalled the terror she felt whenever her husband invited his friends to England to shoot. They came from the Balkans, from France and from Spain and they all had one thing in common. Given a gun they became wild and dangerous. Once armed and in the field they shot at everything that moved, including each other. Lady Cardigan's solution was to get the servants to remove the shot from the cartridges in their bags and replace it with bran. The result was baffled Guns and largely unscathed beaters!

Bear-faced cheek

Bears were a huge problem in India during British rule. In the north of the country they regularly attacked the local people's sheep, grubbed up their crops and occasionally killed a herdsman.

Unlike pheasants and tigers which were shot for sport, food and trophies, the bear was shot whenever possible simply because it was such a nuisance, but a bear was a tough customer as a number of Victorian sportsmen-writers recalled.

One example – and an extraordinary one at that – of the bear's tenacity will suffice. A British soldier on leave had been shooting for several weeks without much success, when he arrived at a steep and narrow ravine. On a ledge high above the floor of the ravine he spotted, out of the corner of his eye, a foraging bear. He took a shot at it and the bear tumbled off his ledge. The soldier was baffled because his shot was wide and he knew he'd completely missed. Clearly the sheer surprise of the shot had been enough to make the bear lose its footing. The bear fell more than 200 feet bouncing off and into jagged outcrops and having watched all this the soldier was certain that despite his bungled shot the bear would be dead anyway. As it turned out he couldn't have been more mistaken. No sooner had the bear hit the ground than it sprang to its feet and charged. The soldier was very lucky indeed – he was just a few paces from a tree that could easily be climbed. Up in the branches with the bear black with rage a few feet below his dangling legs, he tried to re-load but by the time he'd succeeded the angry bear had disappeared into the bush.

Danger man

A shooting incident recorded back in the 1850s reveals just how danger-

ous shooting can be even when the danger has nothing to do with guns. A Pathan tribesman in one of the most remote parts of Nepal had shot an ibex, but failed to find it among the deep snow corries of the high plateau. When he did finally locate the animal he found that it was high on a rocky ledge above his own village. Delighted, he pushed the ibex over the ledge and it was easily collected by his friends from the village below, but it was now almost dark and he was reluctant to try to retrace his steps for fear of falling. Suddenly the peril of his situation became clear to him because at this altitude he knew that spending a night in the open would almost certainly be fatal. He shouted to the villagers a thousand feet below and all they could do was light fires and shout to him to try to keep him awake.

After a few hours the tribesman fell silent and the villagers feared the worst. Cold makes a man sleepy and despite knowing that if he fell asleep that sleep would be his last the tribesman stuck high on the ledge could not resist the pull of unconsciousness. In the middle of the night he finally slumped into unconsciousness and froze to death.

Buffalo bill

Wealthy British sportsmen who trekked across Africa in search of game during the middle decades of the nineteenth century were often hugely popular with local people for the simple reason that what was shot was then eaten by the beaters and carriers who followed the great man.

The writer William Cotton Oswell spent decades in Africa in search of sporting trophies. But despite his huge experience he almost died on one extraordinary occasion. He had gone out alone just half a mile from his huge camp to scout the area. He was sitting quietly on his horse smoking his pipe when he became aware of a gradually increasing roar. Nothing seemed to be visible across the wide dusty plain but within seconds Oswell realised he had somehow managed to position himself in the direct line of a herd of stampeding buffalo. It was one of the few occasions when Oswell's uncanny instinct for self-preservation failed him. There was nothing to do but strand his ground. Perhaps through sheer good luck or because he refused to panic he survived as the huge animals thundered by just a few feet either side of him and he was left unscathed.

Lion's share

An anonymous Victorian sporting author came close to death on a number of occasions while big game hunting in Africa, but his luckiest escape came while he was on a duck shooting expedition.

He was out riding alone and had shot a few duck when he came too close to a lion that had probably been asleep in an area of thick undergrowth beside the track along which the duck shooter was riding. He had no time to react as the lion simply appeared with no warning and let out a huge roar. He glanced back over his pony's haunches and saw the lion spring at him. The pony reared and then bolted but not before the lion had sunk its claws into the terrified pony's back. The duck shooter was spared a severe mauling because the lion had dug its front claws so far into the pony's back that it could not use them to attack him. In the book he wro te on his return to England the sportsman recalled a brief feeling that he was galloping for at least a few seconds with both the lion and himself on the pony's back. He woke some time later to find himself sprawled in the dust and lion and horse long gone. Extraordinarily he was completely unharmed.

Something fishy

In India in the nineteenth century a favourite pastime was fish shooting and the fish favoured for this most bizarre sport was the murrel, a kind of giant carp.

On leave from his job as a civil servant, an Englishman asked the head man of a remote northern Indian village if he could accompany a murrel shooter for a day. They set off early the next morning, the murrel shooter carrying an ancient British army rifle and some homemade ammunition. The civil servant later wrote that he was astonished at how the murrel shooter used the slow, old gun – slow in the sense that there was a perceptible time lag between pulling the trigger and igniting the powder – to remarkably good effect.

The old man led him to the side of a broad river and climbed a gnarled tree that overhung the water. Here he'd made himself a comfortable seat by hacking out a hollow in a fork of two massive branches and smoothing the sides. The old man climbed into the tree and settled down to wait. The Englishman sat nearby in the shade and smoked his pipe, but was told by the old man that absolute stillness was essential. It seemed like hours before anything happened but just as he was about to drop off to sleep the Englishman noticed a sudden movement in the tree.

Down below the old man in the depths of the green water and hardly moving was what looked like a massive dark pig. The pig – in fact a hefty fish – rose slowly to the surface. There was an almighty bang, the water erupted and clouds of dense smoke filled the air.

Then came the really extraordinary bit – no sooner had his gun gone off than the old man leapt from the tree and dived into the water. When he emerged he was carrying the huge dead fish. The fish was thrown on to the bank after which the old man climbed out of the water picked up the fish and set off for the village.

Royal eccentric

European Royal families were at one time so inbred that they had a tendency far above the average, to produce men and women of extraordinary eccentricity. It is only during the past century and with the development of ideas about genetics that we have come to realise that marrying your relatives produces anything but pure blood.

One of the greatest of all European Royal eccentrics was undoubtedly King Carlos of Portugal (1863-1908). Short, enormously overweight and loathed by his own people, he was eventually assassinated.

Throughout his adult life he visited England often and usually to shoot. He apparently adored the atmosphere of English country houses but had a reputation for behaving outrageously. He was also insufferably arrogant and would tolerate no criticism – hardly surprising as he had surrounded himself from childhood with flatterers and sycophants.

He was constantly being told that if he had devoted himself to music he would have been the equal of Beethoven or Mozart; if he had decided on a career as a painter he would have equalled Michelangelo; a career as a soldier would have shown Napoleon a thing or two.

As he came to believe these things his behaviour became ever more arrogant and his arrogance in the shooting field knew no bounds. This caused a difficulty for his English hosts. As Carlos was a member of the aristocracy they had to be polite to him, but his bad manners appalled a nation that prided itself on behaving impeccably, especially in the shooting field.

His hosts put up with his odd behaviour, his rudeness and his bad manners, but the invitations began to dry up when he decided, at the beginning of a day's pheasant shooting, to shoot his birds from the hip. He tried this for a while and then began shooting first from one shoulder and then from the other or even occasionally from between his legs and all the while he infuriated the Guns on either side of him in the line by continually (and rather badly) singing arias from his favourite operas.

Hill climb

Major Neville Taylor was one of those intrepid Englishmen who travelled the world in search of ever more exotic game but of all the animals he pursued his favourite was the ibex.

Striding about the Himalayas he was a familiar figure in the thickest Scottish tweed, but he soon went native – much to the horror of other Englishmen – by wearing local clothes which he insisted were far better adapted to local conditions.

He wrote about his adventures many years later and was always keen to dwell on one particular incident. High on the mountain he and his sherpas were suddenly overwhelmed by a ferocious snowstorm. The major crept into a narrow fissure in the rock and tried to get some sleep. Soon he was dreaming of ibex and their pursuit and so real did the dream become that, as he dashed across a snow-covered corrie in his mind, he rolled over several times on his rocky bed in the real world and woke to find himself just inches from the edge of the rock face and certain death.

He crept back to his tiny cave and fell asleep again. Still the dreams came and this time he was convinced he was a snow leopard stalking an ibex. The dream was particularly intense he later said because of the thin oxygen at high altitude, but whatever the reason he dreamed his snow leopard dream, and crept ever closer to an unsuspecting ibex. He was prepared to spring and bury his fangs in its throat. Suddenly the ibex looked straight at him and instead of being afraid, as it should have been, to his horror it began to advance towards him and was upon him with one bound. He felt sharp hooves in his back, but managed to seize the beast by the neck while it bleated and he awoke – hitting his head hard against the roof of the cave and realising that in the real world he was gripping real wet wool. What on earth was going on? He ran his hands up to where the horns should have been and realised he had got hold of one of the goats the party took with them for meat and milk!

Bear today, gone tomorrow

Western sportsmen regularly travel to Pakistan even today to shoot wild boar. The locals are delighted because boar are completely unclean according to Islam and cannot therefore be hunted by Muslims. So the boar population thrives and the animals do huge amounts of damage to villagers' crops.

The situation was rather similar in India a century and more ago when bears were far more numerous than they are today.

A young British soldier had spent many seasons hunting in the north of India and had come to love the local traditions, the flora and the fauna. He also became a dedicated, even fanatical bear hunter and on one occasion his passion nearly cost him his life.

He was walking with half-a-dozen beaters tracking a bear through thick jungle when, after about three miles, the tracks disappeared and even the local Puthan tribesmen indicated they would probably have to give up. However, the Englishman was determined to shoot this particular bear as it had already attacked and badly injured two children. The little group decided to make camp, and while the sherpas pitched the tents the Englishman and one of his companions wandered off to explore a nearby cave. Unfortunately they had only just entered the cave when a huge and very angry bear rushed at them. The bear knocked the soldier's companion to the ground and rushed past him and out of the cave.

The soldier discovered that the bear's claw had gone right into his companion's skull, although, despite his injuries, the man was still conscious. The party helped the wounded man back to their base camp some six miles away and they explained to the young soldier that Indian bears when attacked had a curious habit of trying to scalp any human who came within reach.

Several hunters had been found dead with all the hair and skin on their heads neatly removed. The soldier, though he continued to hunt bear for many years, never hunted alone.

Thick elephant head

In India elephants were for centuries the favoured mode of transport for tiger hunts. Some elephants were so experienced that they acted like pointers, stopping dead when they sensed a tiger was nearby. One famous elephant had an almost uncanny ability to do this, but he often waited until he was almost too close to the tigers for comfort and on one occasion it nearly cost him his life.

As the hunting party moved along a particularly narrow ride the elephant stopped dead in its tracks and waved its trunk frantically, indicating the presence of a tiger a little ahead and to the left. Before the hunters could ready themselves two tigers appeared just feet ahead of the party perched on their elephant – a moment later and one of the tigers launched itself at the head of the elephant and clung there, digging its claws deep into the elephant's face.

The enraged elephant roared but astonishingly did not bolt. Instead it reared up shaking the tiger off and giving the hunter just enough time to shoot. The first bullet accounted for one tiger, the second missed its mark.

A few days later the elephant's handler noticed a huge swelling on the beast's head, which grew worse over the days and weeks that followed the incident with the tiger.

The animal became increasingly distressed by the pain and at last its owners called in a vet who lanced the huge infected lump on its head. Astonishingly, as the scalpel went in, out popped a .500 bullet. It was the second of the two bullets fired during the tiger incident weeks earlier.

Bear necessities

The popular image of the bear is of a rather cuddly creature but wild bears are among the most dangerous of all animals. Highly aggressive when threatened they are also very fast moving and determined, as a bear hunter shooting in Canada before the First World War discovered. He found himself stalking a female bear for hours and was within fifty yards of her when he took his shot.

He was using an old but well preserved flintlock rifle. Unluckily the cap was damp and instead of the crisp crack the gun merely fizzed a little.

The bear turned sharply round at the sound of the gun's hammer falling, but could see nothing as the hunter was well hidden behind a large stone. Frantically he fixed a fresh firing cap to his gun, lifted his head carefully above the stone, took aim again and fired. This time the cap went off perfectly but nothing else happened. The bear jumped and looked round again. Once more the bear failed to spot him.

Increasingly terrified the sportsman took out his powder flask and put the maximum amount of powder into the nipple to ensure that when the next cap fired there could be no doubt that the powder would ignite. He also wiped the gun down as best he could to rid it of some of the damp. When he next looked cautiously over the top of the rock the bear was twitching her ears suspiciously in all directions. This would certainly be his last chance. Either he bagged the bear with this shot or she would have a pretty good chance of bagging him.

Again he pushed the rifle up over the stone, drew a bead on the bear's shoulder and slowly squeezed the trigger. This time the cap fired perfectly with a loud crack, but the extra powder in the nipple began to fizz alarmingly. For a few terrifying moments the fizzing continued then, with a loud bang, the gun fired, but by this time the hunter had taken the stock from his shoulder and the bullet soared into the sky.

The bear turned instantly on hearing the noise and saw the flash of burning powder leave the muzzle of the gun. With a roar she charged at the hunter now cowering behind the stone just fifty yards away. Bears are not slow moving animals and the hunter knew that in about six seconds she would reach him and he would be dead.

In less than a second he turned and raced down hill and away from the bear, which thundered across the rough stones toward him roaring continually. A short way down the hill was a small ravine full of snow and it was so steep that in crossing it to get to the bear in the first place the hunter had dug slots for his feet and hands. Now, on the rather more rapid return journey he threw himself on to the snow on his back, lifted legs and feet in the air to reduce the amount of friction and sailed away down the slope faster than the fastest bear could ever gallop. One hundred yards further down, the steep snowy slope levelled out and the hunter came to a halt. He looked back to see the bear standing on the edge of the ravine where he had begun his slide. She looked alternately at him and then back at the spot where she had left her cubs. She seemed half inclined to continue the pursuit but changed her mind and disappeared back up the slope. It was the narrowest escape he'd ever had.

Rogue elephant

No one really knows why an elephant suddenly becomes violent and uncontrollable, but as numerous histories and memoirs record, it is far more common than one might imagine. Indeed elephant mahouts – that is their riders – are kitted out with a mallet and chisel to be used in the event that the elephant goes berserk. The chisel is driven into the animal's skull using the mallet to stop it in its tracks.

Those who attempted to shoot rogue elephants were considered not just brave but also foolhardy for this was dangerous sport indeed – as a young Englishman newly arrived in what was still Ceylon discovered in 1906.

The young man, a Mr Walker, was an estate worker, who by his own admission had became obsessed with the idea of shooting an elephant – something that, despite wide experience of game shooting, he had never tried.

He then happened to see an advertisement inviting 'practised sportsmen' to apply for a licence to shoot a particularly troublesome rogue elephant that was said to frequent village lands in the North Western Province. As the elephant appeared to concentrate his activities just twenty miles from where Mr Walker was stationed the temptation was irresistible. So, armed with the licence and a great deal of confidence Mr Walker set off early one morning. He talked to the locals who were able to point him in the direction of some paddy fields where the elephant had been seen several times in recent days.

He must have felt that luck was with him for no sooner had he arrived than the elephant also arrived. It stood knee-deep in water in the middle of the paddy field waving a long piece of bamboo. Mr Walker, seeing the elephant calmly standing in front of him, wondered why people went on about how difficult and dangerous elephant shooting was. He strode confidently to within about one hundred yards of the elephant, aimed at its head and fired.

The .405 Winchester fired straight and true and there seemed to be a reassuring smack as the bullet struck home. But the elephant hardly seemed to notice anything. It turned and walked unhurriedly into the jungle at the edge of the paddy field. And that was that. Not realising that the .405 was wholly inadequate for the job Walker raced into the jungle after the elephant along with his small party of trackers. Despite searching all day they saw no sign of it.

Walker went home and determined to try again for the same elephant the following week. Embarrassed by his failure he borrowed a .500 Westley Richards and plenty of cordite-loaded cartridges.

Back at the paddy field a week later Walker waited an hour or so and then had the satisfaction of seeing the elephant suddenly reappear. This time the giant animal was more cautious. It stood quietly at the edge of the field and partly hidden from view by thick jungle. Walker decided that enough of its head was visible for a shot and he duly took his chance. Once again the elephant simply turned and disappeared into the jungle. Walker and his tracker followed for miles and were about to give up the chase when they heard the elephant crashing about in the undergrowth just a few hundred yards ahead.

When they came closer to him they realised he was standing in an extremely dense thicket of bushes and bamboo, but by lying down Walker could just make out his legs. In a moment of madness – a moment that nearly cost him his life – Walker then fired at one of the elephant's forelegs. He thought this would disable the animal and that he would then be able to run in and finish him off. But far from being disabled by the shot the elephant was enraged – it seemed to know precisely from which direction the shot had come and Walker could hear it almost immediately begin its charge.

The trackers instantly vanished leaving Walker alone on the path and with several tons of elephant heading towards him at thirty miles an hour. He fled but was convinced that every moment was likely to be his last. Then something extraordinary happened. Walker remembered something he'd read in a book years before. He had nothing left to lose so he thought he'd try it. With the elephant almost on top of him he simply stopped, turned and doubled back passing just a few feet to the side of the elephant.

The elephant clearly noticed nothing and simply carried on in the same direction, the noise of its crashing growing ever fainter. Soon the trackers re-appeared and Walker set off for home astonished at his good fortune. By now he was so horrified by his failure that he would almost have preferred death to defeat. He arranged to try one last time the following weekend.

Armed with the heavy Westley Richards, Walker found himself once again at the paddy field where the whole adventure had begun. He picked up the elephant's track and set off into the jungle. An hour later he found the elephant and killed it cleanly with one shot.

8 Way out West

Bounty hunter

The wide open spaces of America gave the European settlers of the eighteenth and nineteenth century access to extraordinary amounts of game. Most of us are aware of the huge numbers of buffalo shot (often from railway carriages) just for the fun of it and of the fate of the America passenger pigeon – wiped out by trapping and shooting despite being at one time the most populous bird on the planet.

In remote parts of rural America of course trapping and shooting were vital if small communities were to survive. This was particularly true in the newly opened up Wild West where a lack of infrastructure meant that groups and individuals were often thrown entirely on their own resources. Despite huge poverty, families survived and their survival was often attributable in part at least to the fact that they were able to live by what they shot. This idea received a bizarre twist in the mid-1850s when a farmer living in a particularly remote part of Wyoming shot far more than he'd bargained for.

He was out in pursuit of rabbits and other small game when he took a long shot at a deer that had crossed a trackway leading to the nearest small town. He thought he might have hit the deer but could find no trace of it nor any trace of a blood trail. He was about to call it a day and head for home when he noticed a boot sticking out from the rough bushes at the side of the road. The boot had a leg attached and it is easy to imagine the farmer's horror at what he thought he'd done. He was an honest man so he immediately walked the ten miles into town and handed himself in at the sheriff's office. The sheriff and a doctor rode out to where the dead man lay and he was brought back into the town.

It was only when he was laid on a table in the sheriff's office that one of the deputies recognised him. A notorious local outlaw, he had been hunted for more than a year by the sheriff and his men and they were delighted to find that the search was now over.

But their surprise was nothing to compare with the surprise of the farmer who received a handsome reward for shooting a dangerous outlaw!

The ambassador's guinea fowl

The African state of Liberia was one of those diplomatic postings that career civil servants dreaded back in the 1950s, but for the American ambassador Ellis Briggs the posting at least gave him the chance to pursue his passion for shooting.

Hardly had he arrived in the country than he set off with a group of colleagues for the unexplored interior. Once clear of the coastal jungle they reached an enormous area of grassland reaching as far as the eye could see.

The ambassador was convinced he'd stumbled across a wildfowler's paradise. The grass stretched for miles in every direction and locals told him that the area was absolutely seething with duck, guinea fowl and geese. The ambassador duly engaged a team of assistants to carry home the huge numbers of birds he was sure he would bag.

The day started well and the marshes were filled with game, but what no one had told him was that they were also filled with extremely poisonous snakes. Every step became a nightmare and in the end, with only a few birds in the bag, they had to give up although they resolved to return dressed more appropriately. But then a more awkward problem arose. Word had spread that the Americans were paying their beaters so when Briggs arrived at the edge of the savannah for his next outing he found the area filled with thousands of hopeful locals offering their services as beaters. No bird would have hung around for a minute given the number of humans milling about. It took a week for the excitement to die down and the Ambassador's party had to hire a local man to organise the beaters and assistants.

At last they arrived at the duck shooting area properly kitted out in snake-proof clothes and with a sensible number of beaters. This time it was bound to go well. And it did.

The shooting was quite exceptional but with guinea fowl rather than duck or geese. The Liberian guinea fowl, a brown bird about the size of a grouse, is a fast flying, extremely acrobatic bird with enough brains to stay on the ground and run for it unless absolutely forced to fly. What impressed the ambassador most, however, was not the quality of the shooting but the ability of the two dozen local beaters to walk through the dense grass without looking where they were going and with no shoes. Not once was a man bitten despite the snakes that seemed to be everywhere.

Officials from other embassies got to hear about the fabulous shooting trips to the savannah and several diplomats cadged a lift with the American ambassador – one Monrovian shot a hole in the floor of the car, another fired at passing donkeys, telegraph poles and buildings; a Polish official turned up drunk and a Russian stole a French official's trousers. Briggs went back to shooting on his own.

Sioux skills

Before the arrival of Europeans, hundreds of different North American tribes hunted buffalo and other animals for food and for skins to make clothes, to keep themselves warm and to build their remarkable tee-pees.

Even as they took their land, the European settlers grudgingly accepted that the Indians – as they called the indigenous peoples – were superb hunters. They were also superb strategists and the battle plans of Sitting Bull, for example, are still studied at the American military Academy at West Point.

European fur-trappers, adventurers and hunters all employed the services of native Americans without whom they would quickly have died and at least one hunter remembered with great affection and admiration the extraordinary hunting skills of his Indian companion.

He wrote an anonymous account in a long vanished American newspaper of his experiences. On one occasion he and his companion found themselves with a damaged gun and unable to shoot anything. They were two days ride from a town that could supply them with a new gun and ammunition and the hunter simply assumed they would have to go hungry. He had made the assumption – almost universal in the early nineteenth century – that the possession of a gun automatically gave him superiority over his Indian companion. But when the gun jammed he was forced to rely on doing things the Indian way. He now took second place in the hunt and was astonished at how his companion could detect an animal trail where there seemed absolutely nothing visible on the ground. The Indian tracker could also get to game of all kinds without being detected. At one point he hid inside a wolf skin to get close enough to a herd of buffalo to kill one with a simple bow and arrow.

But what really amazed the European was how quickly, on another occasion, the Indian learned to use his rifle. He gave him a brief account of how the gun worked and allowed him to try a few shots. With only open sights to rely on he was able to hit the smallest birds at great distances.

'I felt like giving up,' wrote the anonymous tracker, 'when on another occasion my companion jumped from a rock that was at least ten feet above the ground and fired my rifle at a bird while he was still falling through the air. He killed it instantly. It was a feat of marksmanship I knew I could never hope to match.'

Out of the cold

Shooting in remote parts of North America in winter can be a dangerous business – not so much because the hunter is likely to be attacked by his prey but more because the weather can be so dreadful. Sudden fogs or snowstorms can disorientate even the most experienced hunter and very cold weather quickly chills and confuses. Many hunters have lost their lives simply through cold and exhaustion.

One hunter who might easily have died from the cold found a most extraordinary – and inventive way to save his life. He was shooting towards the end of a very cold November and had almost given up when he spotted an elk just a few hundred yards away. He took a quick shot and the elk fell immediately. When the hunter went to the spot where the elk appeared to have fallen there was nothing to be seen. But a few yards further on and a few drops of blood told him that the animal had been hit. He began tracking it across the snowy featureless landscape. Darkness was falling when, almost two hours later, he found the elk dead at the edge of a frozen stream. He was delighted but his pleasure turned to fear within minutes as it was clear from the sky overhead and from the deteriorating weather that a serious snowstorm was on the way.

Within minutes the fierce wind was driving snow horizontally into his face. Landmarks were quickly obliterated. He found himself in the gathering darkness miles from the nearest house and with not a bush or a tree anywhere in sight. Darkness fell and the storm if anything became worse. He knew that in the sub-zero temperatures and blinding snow there was no way he could find his way back to safety and he could feel the cold beginning to penetrate so deeply that he was in danger of frostbite. Then he had an idea. Years earlier he had read a wonderful hunting book in which the author had survived a freezing night in the open by sheltering inside an animal he had shot.

Quickly the hunter gralloched his elk and dragged the carcase to the leeward side of a large rock. He then squeezed as much of himself as he could inside the still-warm body cavity of the elk so that on one side he was hemmed in by the rock and on the other surrounded by elk fur and elk fat. Despite temperatures way below freezing he survived an extremely uncomfortable night. By the time dawn came, the snowstorm was over and he was able to walk the three miles back to his vehicle, collect his deer and head for home, but it had been a close-run thing.

Helicopter shots

The American ambassador Ellis Briggs seems to have worked in every country where it was worth working if you happened to be a keen shooting man – South America, Europe and most places in between. But Korea seems to have been something special. Apart from a fascinating trip in search of wild swans Korea gave him the chance to try out some novel not to say bizarre shooting techniques – top of the list in terms of sheer eccentricity has to be the time he organised a group of helicopters to drive duck.

This started out as a scientific study into a new cold weather suit developed by the United States military. The ambassador seems to have got sufficiently involved with the project to try out the suit. It was made of what seemed to be foam runner and plastic and, like a wetsuit, it was skin tight and covered the wearer from ankle to neck. However cold the weather the suit was supposed to be sufficient weather protection on its own, or at least that was the theory.

Immediately he tried on the suit the ambassador found it was like being in an oven – which should not have been a problem as the suit was fitted with numerous ingenious vents.

However, the real test of the suit was to be conducted along Korea's Han River, a place of extreme cold in winter. The idea was to fly the ambassador and one or two other top officials – also dressed in the new suit – by helicopter, which was the only way in to the area at that time. In return for testing the suit the ambassador persuaded the military authorities to let him try shooting duck out of the window of the helicopter.

The theory was this. You sat in the helicopter's plastic bubble – in other words in the main body of the thing – but with the right door removed. The pilot flew along until the chopper was alongside a cruising flock of mallard and the ambassador would then try to shoot them. If a duck went down the helicopter would land to pick it up.

When the three helicopters arrived in the Han valley the men trying out the suits would be dropped on a giant ice-floe where they would be left for several hours to test the suits. While they waited to be picked up the idea was that they would amuse themselves by shooting at any passing duck.

As the ambassador boarded his helicopter he was told by the pilot not to shoot upwards or to take any shots when either of the other helicopters was alongside. High shots, as the pilot pointed out, would make nasty holes in the helicopter's rotor blades, which might mean an unscheduled and very rapid descent. Those who'd shot from the chopper before – or so the ambassador was told – normally stepped partly out of the helicopter and put one foot on its ski. The ambassador thought he might give this technique a miss.

They took off, flying two hundred feet above the river. Soon they were matching the speed of a big flock of duck, but try as he might the ambassador couldn't hit a thing. He tried shooting further and further ahead of the lead duck hoping to allow for the speed of the helicopter, but it was no good.

At the end of the day he talked to a colonel who regularly shot duck from the helicopter and was told that he should have fired about one hundred feet ahead of any duck to have the least chance of hitting it. Theoretically this should not have been necessary as duck and helicopter were travelling at the same speed, but the problem was a mystery that would never be solved. The ambassador resolved to give it another go if the chance ever arose – it never did. But the trip hadn't been entirely wasted. He was able to report that the Michelin-man suit he'd been trying out was unbearably hot and was likely to be a complete waste of time anywhere other than at the South Pole.

Ghost swamp

The remote swamps of Louisiana still retain a great deal of French character from the days of the earliest settlers. French Creole is still spoken in some areas and Cajun cooking betrays its European origins. When the French settlers arrived in the eighteenth century they found a wild untamed environment, which was rife with malaria and other diseases but also rich in wildlife.

A letter from Louisiana that found its way back to a Paris newspaper described one of the more bizarre goings on in a place that, over the years, developed a reputation unique in America. There was always talk of obeah or voodoo and many swamp dwellers reported hallucinations caused by endless fevers and lonely isolated lives.

It may have been the result of fever or disease but the letter that reached Paris from Louisiana was certainly bizarre. It concerned a man who had lived alone in the swamps for more than twenty years. He was a keen shooting man who was often seen out on the marshes in his punt shooting duck and other birds. No one ever visited his remote hut but occasionally another fowler would punt across to the old man's boat and ask him how he was getting along. He was usually friendly but guarded and always denied that he had managed to shoot anything. Those who saw him also noticed how strange his clothes had become. He went without shoes and wore a hat made from duck skin but with the bird's head still in place. His coat was a badly prepared animal skin and he clearly hadn't shaved or washed for years. When other gunners watched him they marvelled at his skill as a shot but were baffled by his almost complete lack of any need for company.

Years passed and then one day a gunner who knew the swamp as well as any man came across the old gunner's hut. It was badly dilapidated and clearly hadn't been used for a number of years. There was no sign at all of the old man. Soon word spread that the old man had probably died. In the treacherous swamp he might easily have fallen into the water and been unable to get out again. Within hours his body would have been eaten by the various creatures that inhabited the swamp. A few months passed and then a gunner reported seeing the old man in his usual punt waiting for the duck. He tried shouting across to the old man but there was no reaction. He decided to go over and talk to him. As he manoeuvred his punt he had to detour around a reed bed on the other side of which the old man's punt should have been lying. As he cleared the reed bed he was astonished to discover no trace of the old gunner or his boat. He went home and assumed it must have been a trick of the light or perhaps the old man, not wanting to be disturbed, had simply set off for home. A week later and in the same spot he saw the old man again and tried to reach him but each time he neared the spot the old man and his boat would somehow vanish. Sightings of the old man continued on and off for a year or two but no one ever managed to get close enough to speak to him. Then at last it was over and neither the old man nor his punt was ever seen again.

Bouncing Czech

In Communist Czechoslovakia during the 1960s there came each year to the American embassy an invitation to shoot. For a keen shooting man like the ambassador it was difficult to resist because the venue was the old Hapsburg hunting lodge at Zidlochovice.

Each Gun was told to bring at least eight hundred rounds of ammunition – the Communists were going to show these Americans that the Czechs could produce much bigger and therefore better shooting than any decadent capitalist.

Zidlochovice, some one hundred and fifty miles east of Prague, had for centuries been the sporting preserve of the Hapsburg kings. It was famous for huge bags of pheasants and for being close to the site of the Battle of Austerliz, which was fought just a little beyond the end of the vast estate forests.

The lodge at Zidlochovice was monumental in scale and also monumentally uncomfortable – too cold in winter and too hot in summer. Every room – and the rooms were vast –was filled with trophies. It was almost as if the Communists had to outdo their aristocratic hunting forebears. Statues of bad-tempered looking Stalin were everywhere among the vast numbers of wall to wall deer trophies, almost as if the heads were not deer at all but the heads of his victims.

As it turned out, the day's shooting was as vast as the lodge and as uncomfortable. It was also run with absurdly militaristic precision. A trumpeter blasted the guests out of bed at 6am and the ambassador had a sense of foreboding when he shouldered his bag of eight hundred cartridges – it was almost too heavy for one man to carry at all let alone comfortably.

A speech filled with stern warnings was designed to ensure that the Guns knew what they could and could not do – the threat of the Gulag seemed to hang over everything – and then they were off.

Each shoot day of the season involved using at least three hundred local farmer beaters and there were so many shoot days that the estate produced more than forty thousand birds a season – a figure that would be an embarrassment at any English shoot.

Absurdly the American ambassador noticed as they gathered outside the lodge that there were secret policeman everywhere. They hadn't even had the sense to change out of their cheap city overcoats and city shoes which were already stained badly with mud. The American ambassador thought they seemed extremely ill at ease probably because here at least they could not arrest anyone for subverting the aims of the revolution (or whatever) simply because all those doing the shooting were diplomats with diplomatic immunity.

Each man shooting was supplied with a man to carry his guns, another man to carry his cartridges and a boy with a pad and pencil to keep his score. Each man shooting also had a team of three city dressed secret service men attached to him.

They were warned not to shoot boar or deer, but anything else was fair game and then it was time for the off – or at least it was time once the officials had persuaded the Argentine ambassador that he would not need his revolver.

There were ten diplomats shooting and they were taken to a section of forest where ten dark rides were cut through the dark trees before disappearing over the horizon. Ambassadors got the best lanes (the ones in the middle) while lesser ranking officials were assigned to the outer rides. As the Guns walked along their rides there would be dozens of beaters keeping pace with them on either side through the thick woods putting the birds up – at least that was the theory.

Then the ambassador realised that so obsessed with control were the officials that he was to be allowed only to shoot when his loader decided to load the gun. When he asked if he could perform this little task for himself it was made abundantly clear that this would not be acceptable. The incongruous little group moved off into their ride and perhaps at some unseen signal from the secret service men, the ambassador's gun bearer suddenly took two cartridges from the ammunition man. He loaded the gun and handed it to the ambassador. A pheasant got up a few yards further on and the gun bearer, the scorer, the ammunition carrier and the secret service policemen all bellowed 'Shoot!'

Flustered by the roars of the crowd the ambassador missed and the scorer shouted 'Zero' and marked the poor man's scorecard appropriately. Several similar shots followed and though rattled by the extraordinary circumstances in which he found himself, the ambassador eventually managed to shoot a hen pheasant. He was then told that hens were not allowed and he was told much as a naughty five year old would be told off for failing to tidy his bedroom.

And so it continued for mile after mile through the forest. The ambassador was never allowed to handle a single cartridge and he had to endure a permanent and voluble audience of six who screamed either 'Zero!' or 'Hen' or 'Don't shoot!' at every opportunity.

The loudest shouts came from the three secret service policemen. The ambassador, too diplomatic to say anything, was beginning to get extremely annoyed, particularly at the three secret service policemen who looked out of place and were easily the most annoying members of an incredibly annoying group.

The ambassador decided to teach the spooks a lesson. When a hare ran on ahead of him he paused hoping the hare would do that strange thing that driven hares often do – double back on itself. Clearly the gods were with the ambassador for having run fifty feet forward the hare did a u-turn and ran back and almost through the ambassador's legs. He waited until it had reached the three secret service policemen and knowing full well that shooting behind was not permitted, turned and fired between the second and the third policemen and well above the hare's head.

The policemen threw themselves on the ground while the scorer shouted 'Good shooting!'

But the shot had the desired effect. The policemen kept much further back and made no further comment on the ambassador's shooting.

A little more relaxed by now, the ambassador got into his swing and when the walked up shooting was over and the Guns tried shooting from pegs he knocked thirty-eight birds out of the sky in just fifteen minutes. But, as he said later, this was not actually that much of an achievement as the sky was continually black with birds

At the end of that one day ten diplomats had shot one thousand four hundred and fifty pheasants, together with seven hundred hares and more than three hundred rabbits. Several of the diplomats, who had fired almost continually for more than five hours, had smashed fingers, dislocated arms and severe shoulder bruising.

Most of the game from Zidlochovice was not, sadly, sent off to be consumed by the workers in distant factories and farms – it was sent to the west as quickly as possible in exchange for hard currency. But on the day of the ambassador's shoot the officials insisted that all the game belonged to the people of Czechoslovakia and that it was going to the west because that was the will of the people.

Going, going gone

Eating sandwiches and sipping Jack Daniels whiskey in the Korean countryside an American visitor had been encouraged to go out in pursuit of wild swans. These were hugely prolific around the estuary of the Naktong River along whose sides the rice paddies spread as far as the eye could see.

The ambassador and his friends waited expectantly until they heard the far off sounds of a deep and unmistakable booming; the swans, hundreds of them, were coming. High up across the wide expanse of the mudflats but still miles away they could see arrow-shaped formations heading steadily towards them.

The deep thrumming noise grew ever louder as the birds approached and it was a sight the visitor was never to forget. These were wild swans flying south from the ice-bound Siberian winter. In this quiet corner of Korea they spent their time feeding out at sea during the daytime before flying inland at evening to the estuary to roost.

The American team watched the birds land on the distant estuary and decided to try for them. They headed for the sea wall and then, under instruction from their guide, they fanned out in a line keeping well down and out of sight.

The idea was that their guide would then move carefully round until he was behind the swans and well away from the line of Guns. He would then fire a shot hoping the birds would rise and head away from the sound of his shot and towards the waiting Guns. From previous attempts to drive the swans the guide knew that they would circle and then head to the sea wall. He explained to the Americans that they should on no account show themselves or fire until the last possible moment.

But the Guns were in for a shock – when they asked their guide how well previous shooting parties had fared they were told that despite the birds lifting from the estuary and circling as predicted, previous attempts to shoot them had all been completely unsuccessful. Their guide had absolutely no idea why this had happened but admitted that he'd never managed to shoot a swan himself.

The American had estimated that several hundred swans were lying out on the estuary and his hopes of bagging a bird were high. Time seemed to pass at a painfully slow rate and one or two of the Guns were beginning to nod off, when suddenly a sharp crack roused them to their senses. The guide, now some miles distant, had fired his shot and the huge flocks of birds were moving clumsily but with increasing noise and speed along the water and up into the air, their heavy bodies only reluctantly rising in flight. Once in the air, their clumsiness seemed gradually to disappear and soon they were climbing steadily into a startlingly blue sky.

Just as predicted the birds soon moved into a tight formation and began to turn and it was a turn that would bring them directly over the waiting Guns. Everything went according to plan and as the birds passed overhead each of the team managed to fire both barrels. To everyone's amazement the birds carried on as if nothing had happened. They'd apparently been within range, yet none appeared to have been hit. A voice shouted: 'My God those birds must be armour plated! How could we all have missed?'

They were still debating their failure when their guide returned from his long journey round the estuary. Their mouths dropped open when they saw that he was carrying a large dead swan.

By a million to one chance the shot he'd fired – and with a rifle! – to put the swans up off the water had skimmed like a flat pebble and scored a bull's eye on one of the most distant swans as it sat unconcerned on the water.

A good ducking

The early 1930s were a tough time in the United States. The Great Depression had made life extremely hard for millions of Americans and as times became ever tougher, the old frontier spirit re-asserted itself and Americans increasingly took up sporting shooting to put something on the table. The great American tradition was for the lone hunter to wander the woods and prairies. Driven shooting in the English sense was largely unknown which is hardly surprisingly given that America is blessed with wide open spaces and England is not.

But despite this, Americans do enjoy shooting together and to avoid shooting each other by accident they tend to wear bright colours and tell each other where they are planning to go. Despite every precaution there are of course on occasion near misses, including some quite remarkable ones.

Two elderly Americans were shooting from a double battery – a kind of enclosed metal boat. It was anchored up offshore and they were concealed in the special compartments in which the gunners lie until the game is in sight.

It was early morning, absolutely silent and icy cold, but the gunners had high hopes that a good solid party of duck would soon be arriving. They'd prepared the area carefully by putting out wooden decoy duck all around their battery and all the signs were good for a great day's sport. Great South Bay, a noted wildfowl area, had been one of their favourite shooting spots for decades and they knew its every mood. The plan, as ever, was to wait until a party of duck was committed to landing among the fake duck and then spring up from their hidden compartment and let them have it. The plan seemed foolproof.

Suddenly the sound of wing beats alerted the two men who immediately showed themselves and, picking a target each, fired. The duck rose in a roar of wing splashes and general chaos.

Mr Scott, the first of the two men to fire, had aimed at a bird that had risen just a couple of feet from the water. Mr Simpson fired at a bird well up in the air. Mr Scott was about to fire his second barrel when the bird he was aiming at crumpled and fell into the water. Yet Mr Scott knew he hadn't managed to fire at it.

From damage to his gun Mr Scott quickly realised what had happened. Just as he'd been about to fire at his low bird, Mr Simpson, swinging his gun to catch up with the higher bird had fired and hit Mr Scott's gun barrels about six inches from the muzzle. The shot struck the right barrel a glancing blow, broke through the wall of the barrel and then continued along the inside of that barrel and out the end. The gun being already aimed at a duck the shot travelled out of the muzzle in exactly the right direction to bring down the bird that Mr Scott had been aiming at all the time.

Bear waiting

North American and Canadian sportsmen know as much as anybody that a local guide is vital to a good day's shooting, which is why, traditionally, they would engage the services of locals or, better still, native Americans who had an almost instinctive ability to track game.

In British Columbia in the early part of the twentieth century, the writer Frantz Rosenberg always took Indian trackers with him. They hardly ever failed when it came to locating game and one or two became friends with Rosenberg. Indeed during one long shooting season Rosenberg got so close to one of his trackers that the man told him a remarkable story. There had been several terrible winters in the United States of America during the last decade of the nineteenth century when the tracker was growing up. During one particularly savage December the tribe to which the tracker belonged was camped on the Stickine River. Their winter hunt had failed almost completely and there was a very real danger that many of the women and children would die of starvation – they simply had no stores of food. The once great herds of buffalo and

caribou that for so long had sustained them were gone, all but wiped out by European settlers who shot them by the thousand from passing trains just for the fun of it.

At the edge of despair the tribal elders decided to send one of their strongest hunters to scout around the area and see if he could find anything. The hunter wandered for miles up higher and higher into the forest and without warning, as he later told the tale, he found himself confronted by a huge grizzly bear. Even if he managed to shoot it before it got to him the hunter knew that he would never be able to carry the meat back down to the tribe, but then something strange happened. The bear showed no signs of aggression and began instead to walk around the hunter down towards the river. The hunter followed until the bear came close to the camp. Only then did he kill the bear. Then there was enough meat for all and the tribe was saved. There seemed to be no explanation other than that the bear had sacrificed itself for the tribe.

The tracker who told Rosenberg the story insisted that animals, like men, would sometimes sacrifice themselves in this way.

Lion tamer

The wealthy American industrialist Stewart Edward White hunted in Africa in the early years of twentieth century. He was immensely rich and immensely find of trophy hunting. His plan was to bag at least one each of all the big species – lion, tiger, leopard, black rhino, white rhino and elephant – and he travelled widely across most of Africa and Asia to do it. He narrowly avoided death on several occasions, but was the first to admit that the most extraordinary thing he'd seen while out shooting was an unarmed African villager attacking an enraged lion.

White out in search of game with the villager – who knew every inch of the bush for miles round their camp – they found themselves on a well worn path close to a village where they were planning to stop for lunch. Without a word the villager, who was about ten feet ahead of White, suddenly stopped and remained absolutely motionless.

He didn't signal to White, but from the sudden way the man had stopped and his absolute rigidity, the American knew instantly that they were an inch from disaster of some kind. The American assumed the villager had seen a lion or buffalo. Hoping to get a shot at whatever it was the American worked his way slowly around the African keeping as low as possible and wherever possible under or behind what little cover there was.

After a few moments he had reached a position where he could at least see what was happening – he saw a huge male lion sitting on its haunches and staring directly at the African from just a dozen or so yards. Neither man nor animal moved a muscle.

Time seemed to stand still and then the African did something that made the American think he must have gone completely mad. He leaned forward until his downward stretching hands were about a foot from the ground, while tilting his head back in order to maintain eye contact with the lion. He then began a sort of crouching shuffle towards the lion. White probably should have tried a shot at the animal since it was sitting absolutely still, but he was so astonished at what was happening that he remained frozen to the spot. If the truth were known he was probably also fascinated by the extraordinary dance the African seemed to be performing.

When the shuffling man had reduced the distance between him and the lion by about half, the animal, which until then had maintained an absolute stillness, began to swish its tail. It then broke off eye contact and looked for some time to one side almost as if it was afraid to meet the unrelenting gaze of the African. Twenty paces were left between the African and the lion when, in the time it takes to blink, the lion turned on its heel and fled.

White talked for a long time to the African who maintained that in his village all the men, women and children knew that if they encountered a lion the trick he had just performed was their only real chance of surviving the encounter. The man would not be drawn on whether or not it was always successful.

White's exploits led him into many a dangerous escapade and his books are filled with stories of extraordinary escapes, but he was clearly most impressed by examples of unarmed people finding skilful ways to avoid or deflect dangerous animals. There are numerous reports of unarmed Africans escaping what would normally have been certain death, but few of these are stranger than the tale of one of White's bearers

who was caught off-guard by an angry buffalo. The animal had clearly already been attacked when the bearer stumbled across it and of course the buffalo was in no position to distinguish between this harmless human and one, now long gone, who fired an annoying arrow which was still stuck in its flank. No sooner had the buffalo spotted the young man than it charged and he, being unarmed, simply ran for it.

A buffalo in a rage is reputedly an unstoppable animal and the bearer must have known that in seconds it would catch him and trample him to death. There were no trees to climb so the bearer with great presence of mind threw himself into a shallow depression that was half concealed by a rock. The buffalo stopped dead at the depression and tried to get the man with his horns, but it could only do this by putting its head down and then rooting carefully about in the narrow gap where the man lay. As soon as the buffalo's nose was within reach the bearer grabbed it and gave it a fearful wrench. The buffalo's nose is extremely sensitive and with a bellow of pain it lifted its head and ran as fast as it could from what it probably thought was an enormous bee.

9 Dog Days

Seal of approval

Until well into the nineteenth century visitors to Scotland and the West Country of England often went seal shooting. Such sport would be frowned on now but a century and more ago seal numbers were high and local fishermen believed the seals took too many fish and were very happy to see them shot.

The technique was to shoot them with a rifle but in such a way that the dead seal didn't sink. The best way to do this was to shoot the seal on land but the difficulty was that often even a mortally wounded seal had enough energy to throw itself into the water where it immediately sank and was unrecoverable. Occasionally, for reasons no one could quite make out, a seal would fall into the water and not sink. In these cases the shooter would often set off in a rowing boat to retrieve the seal but with the fast tides that poured through the rock channels off the North coast of Scotland this could be a tricky operation.

On one remarkable day – according to a report that later appeared in a local newspaper – what should have been a tricky operation almost turned into a tragedy.

It began when an English sportsman shot a seal that seemed to be well back from the water's edge. Unfortunately the seal had enough life left in it to reach the sea where it dived and vanished. Cursing his luck the man who had fired the shot was considering packing up for home when, moments later, the seal floated to the surface. It was certainly dead but already a couple of hundred yards from the shore.

He set off over the rocks towards the boat that was kept in a small boathouse at a point where a small stream entered the sea. Luckily the boat was moored in precisely the direction in which the seal was drifting. Just as he reached the boat the man realised his spaniel was missing. He ran back over the rocks shouting and whistling but there was no sign of her. He thought she had probably gone off in search of rabbits but this was not like her at all.

Assuming she was safe and determined to bring back the seal he launched the boat and began rowing furiously out to sea and toward the now distant speck of seal. He was probably half a mile from the shore when he stopped rowing and checked the position of the seal through his binoculars. He then noticed a tiny flurry at the side of the dead animal as if it were being attacked by a small shoal of fish.

He began rowing again and was soon close enough to get a really good look at the seal and, to his astonishment, he saw clinging to the seal's neck his cocker spaniel. She was dwarfed by the seal but had clearly decided that she would try to retrieve it and despite the fact that she had now drifted almost a mile offshore she was still determined not to let go! On reaching the seal he pulled the dog aboard by the scruff of the neck and then roped the seal's tail to the back of the boat. Against the tide it was a long, exhausting journey back to the shore pulling the heavy seal. The dog slumped exhausted in the well of the boat and he realised that if he had not caught up with the seal the dog would certainly have continued to hold on until she drowned from exhaustion so determined was she to retrieve what her master had shot.

Name game

A keeper who worked on an English aristocrat's estate had just rounded up the Guns at the end of a drive in which the shoot owner's dogs – skilfully worked by the keeper – had successfully collected all the birds. A visiting Gun was so impressed that he pointed to the biggest of the three dogs and shouted across to the keeper:

'What's the name of that dog?'

'I know,' came the keeper's reply.

'I dare say you do, you impudent man,' came the Gun's riposte. 'Or I shouldn't have asked.'

'What about that spotty one,' he tried again. 'What's his name?'

'You know,' came the exasperating reply.

'If I damn well knew I shouldn't have asked,' said the Gun, who was becoming very cross. Turning to a fellow guest he said: 'I can see I'll have to knock this fellow's head off for his cheek if I don't get a satisfactory answer soon.' There was a third dog so he decided to try once more.

'What about him? Yes, the one nearest you now?'

'Ask him,' came the infuriating reply.

'Damn me if I don't get you turned out of your place for this infernal insolence,' said the Gun who was very aristocratic and very angry.

But when the owner of the shoot, who also owned the keeper's three dogs, turned up he laughed long and loud on hearing his distinguished guest's complaint.

'I don't think you quite understand,' he said. 'Old Joe wasn't being in the least bit rude. In fact I am entirely to blame because the dogs' names are I No, U No and Axum.'

Sleeping partner

Where would we be without our dogs? Half the pleasure of shooting is the companionship of a good dog – which may explain why many of us are happy to spend a small fortune on a top quality Labrador or spaniel. Most dogs will keep working until they drop, but there are numerous hilarious – and occasionally extraordinary – stories of dogs who decided it was really time they did their own thing.

One of the most famous shooting dog stories concerned a splendid animal owned by a close friend of King Edward VII. Not wanting to be disgraced by a poor animal in such illustrious company, the king's friend made sure he bought the best dog that money could buy: it was fully trained and came from a long line of excellent gundogs. Its new owner was assured that it would behave impeccably yet on its first day in the field the dog vanished almost as soon as the first drive had begun. It pricked up its ears at the sound of the beaters and disappeared into the nearest woodland.

The dog re-appeared at lunchtime and re-joined its master as if nothing had happened until the shooting started again in the afternoon. Then it disappeared again and despite a great deal of searching it could not be found until about three o'clock when the final shots died away and the last drive came to an end.

Loathe to give up on a dog with such a fine pedigree, the owner took it to other shoots where his fellow Guns were less exalted. But wherever they went precisely the same thing happened and the dog, once gone, could never be found.

At last by sheer good fortune the dog's secret was discovered. A beater who had stayed well behind the other beaters after hurting his foot saw a dog creeping through the field the beaters had just crossed and dropping into a nearby ditch. The beater hobbled over and found the dog curled up, fast asleep and snoring loudly. And there it slept until some sixth sense told it lunch was in the offing at which time it woke up and headed back to its master.

After this discovery numerous attempts were made to curb the dog's terrible habit but all failed. Kept on a leash and attached to the Gun's peg the dog showed every interest in proceedings but as soon as it was turned loose to retrieve a bird it immediately ran off and could only rarely be found. Soon the owner gave up and kept the dog as a pet so while other dogs worked hard in all weathers for their keep this crafty animal stayed permanently at home curled up in front of the fire.

A pig of a gundog

In the nineteenth century, particularly in Britain, numerous breeds of dog were used for retrieving: these included setters and pointers, Labradors and spaniels. Some once-famous breeds have all but vanished. The Clumber spaniel, for example, was an enormously popular gundog as was the flatcoat retriever. Both are rarely seen today.

Spaniels have come to dominate among those Guns who want a dog that will root out game; Labradors, perhaps the most popular gundog of all time, are the reverse – superb when it comes to retrieving, but less useful when game has to be hunted out.

But the modern shooter who tends inevitably to choose between these two breeds is forgetting the history of dogs and sport, for our ancestors were far more inclined to try pretty much any dog breed. Mongrels were often used as gundogs and with success. Other breeds that were once used to put up pheasants are still with us but they are known only as delightful pets – few realise for example that the poodle was bred as a shooting dog and in its day it was one of the most highly regarded.

Davy Peters grew up with an all-consuming passion for shooting, fishing and hunting. He was also a genius with animals who, it was said, could turn any dog into a gundog. He trained terriers and basset hounds to bring his birds back and he once had a bull-mastiff that could compete with the best spaniel in the land.

Then one day at a famous estate in Yorkshire he turned up for what was to be one of the most extraordinary day's shooting ever seen.

Instead of arriving on horseback or in a carriage like the other gentleman Gunners, he trotted down the lane to the place where the Guns were to meet on a well-trained and apparently docile bull.

The massive animal, complete with a specially made halter that enabled Davy to steer him, was followed by six full-grown pigs. Each answered instantly to its name when, from his precarious position high on the bull's back, Davy roared commands at the top of his voice. While the various guests stood around drinking and waiting for the off, Davy's highly trained pigs kept close to him and warned off any intruding Labradors or spaniels. When the guests set off for the first drive Davy left his bull tethered in the yard and stalked off across the fields with his six pigs close at heel. One or two other Guns became embarrassed at their own occasionally unruly hounds for Davy's pigs were models of good, disciplined behaviour. When the shooting began several of Davy's companions forgot to shoot so astonished were they by the antics of his pigs. When Davy toppled a bird out of the sky he would choose a pig to collect it and obediently the pig named would dash off, pick up the bird and return it to his master's feet. As the day wore on and the guests moved from drive to drive the pigs were used one after another in strict rotation.

For years after Davy always took one or more of his pigs shooting – 'They've more brains in their trotters than most dogs have in their heads,' he used to say when asked about his unusual companions. Davy's exploits in the shooting field made him famous and eventually he was invited to court. There must have been gasps of astonishment at the Palace when Davy replied to the invitation by saying he couldn't possibly come as he was busy training an otter to fish for him.

But Davy wasn't the only shooting man who believed in pig power. In the 1860s a Mr Toomer – apart from his name we know little about him – became well known in the New Forest in Hampshire for teaching a pig to retrieve game, but having successfully done this Mr Toomer decided to go a little further and teach the pig to point game as well. He spent months using a special system of rewards and chastisement and his pig gradually realised what she was being asked to do. On a never to be forgotten day one frosty December she found and pointed fifteen pheasants and then retrieved them once her master had shot them. It was the first time she hadn't run in too soon. Toomer was delighted, but he soon lost interest and tried to teach a deer to do the same thing. He spent years working with a young fallow and although she never learned to retrieve game she apparently was able to point quite successfully.

Trouting Labrador

An elderly shooting man who was still a regular at the local shoot well into his nineties, always insisted on taking two or three dogs with him. The dogs seemed almost as ancient as he was himself and one of them – the old man's favourite – had lost the use of its back legs. Nothing daunted the old man had commissioned a blacksmith friend to make a set of light-weight wheels attached to two shafts that were strapped to the dog's back. After initial problems the dog got the idea and began to race about again like a puppy. Its owner quickly realised that the dog's retrieving abilities would be even further enhanced if the wheels were fitted with a suspension system. Once again the blacksmith got to work and soon the dog was winning an occasional local retrieving competition as well as picking up regularly on local shoots. The old man was delighted and the dog led an active life far beyond what would normally be expected for a Labrador.

The old man was clearly something of an eccentric because in addition to building wheels for one Labrador he taught another to retrieve not birds or rabbits or hares but fish.

The technique was simple. The old man would hook a trout and play it until it was almost ready for the net. Then, instead of using a net, he would whistle to his dog and it would dive into the river, grab the fish and leap out delivering it neatly to hand. The old man insisted it saved him the back-breaking business of carrying a net and it gave the Labrador plenty of exercise. But there were drawbacks. Eventually the dog insisted on waiting in the river rather than on the bank until its master had hooked a fish. It also became hopeless at retrieving birds!

Egg surprise

Anyone who has watched gundogs in action at a field trial will have been astonished at their intelligence, so perhaps it is not surprising that many

gundog owners have taught their animals to do remarkable things, but few dogs can have mastered the trick a Victorian sportsman taught his Labrador.

He was a keen shooting man who regularly shot duck on the lakes and ponds on his farm. One lake had a small island in the middle on which the ducks often laid their eggs. Now this shooting man enjoyed eating duck eggs but didn't have a boat on the lake and so had no easy way to reach the nests.

Then he had an idea. He decided he would try to train one of his gundogs to swim across to the lake and retrieve the eggs without breaking them. Months later after numerous disasters the dog finally realised what was wanted. It had long ago got the hang of retrieving the eggs. The problem was to stop it eating them! A juicy piece of beef used as a reward for success eventually persuaded the dog that it was better delicately to retrieve the egg rather than crush and eat it and from that day on the dog was frequently sent across to the lake whenever his master needed an egg for breakfast. In fact with repeated retrieves the dog would bring a whole nest-full of eggs back one at a time and without a single breakage.

But perhaps the strangest part of the tale is that a year or so after the dog began its occasional egg forays its owner happened to be at the lake very early one morning and he noticed an animal swimming. It was a fox. It is rare to see a fox swimming – unless it's in the process of escaping the hunt – so the man kept as well hidden as possible to see why the animal had taken to the water.

The fox reached the island in the middle of the lake and a few moments later could be seen swimming back with an egg in its mouth. It reached the shore and trotted off into the undergrowth with the egg held delicately in its jaws. Moments later it was back in the water and heading for the island. It made the journey back and forth four times. Each time it took the unbroken egg into the wood – clearly it was returning to its earth to feed its young.

On the fifth journey the fox reached the bank on its return journey and then very deliberately crushed the egg and swallowed it. Clearly the cubs had been fed, the nest was now empty and the fox needed its own breakfast!

The intriguing question was: had the fox been watching the labrador swim to the island and simply copied it?

Hot dog

Some cultures dislike or even loathe dogs, but the British at least have always had the sense to recognise their extraordinary abilities. From bomb disposal to drug searches and rescue work, dogs are invaluable, which is why we have a long tradition of affection for man's best friend. In the shooting world dogs have rescued people from drowning, gone for help when their masters have had heart attacks or been injured in some way and, of course, helped in the day to day business of retrieving sportsmen's birds that in many cases might otherwise have been lost. A story in a mid-nineteenth century newspaper published in Middlesex records the exploits of what must be one of the most extraordinary dogs that ever lived.

A keeper called Hale –we are never told his first name – owned Bosun and the dog's brief period of fame, which came via the newspaper columns, was not brought about as a result of one particular act of intelligence but rather a lifetime of brilliance in the field.

The keeper told the newspaper that when he'd chosen Bosun as a puppy he had sensed there was something special about him. 'He was lively and had such a knowing look about him,' said Hale.

Bosun learned quickly to retrieve and was a star performer at every pheasant shoot, rarely failing to find a bird. He was also lightning quick. When Bosun was only eighteen months old, Hale was walking near the big house on the estate when he met a servant who explained that the house was in an uproar as the three-year-old daughter of the owners had gone missing. Her parents were frantic.

Having no certain idea that it would help, Hale offered to use Bosun to search for the child. A piece of the child's clothing was found, Bosun sniffed it and immediately set off with Hale close behind. Hale later said that it was if Bosun had suddenly discovered he had a bloodhound gene in him.

The dog refused to be distracted from its mission as it criss-crossed a nearby wood moving gradually further away from the house. This continued for nearly an hour before the dog suddenly went into reverse and headed quickly back toward the house. A few hundred yards from home Bosun dived into an old ha-ha, or ditch. At the end of the ditch the little girl was found. She was fast asleep, scratched by brambles and covered in mud but otherwise unharmed. Bosun and Hale were greeted as heroes up at the house and Hale's wages were immediately increased.

Word quickly spread of Bosun's extraordinary success and Hale was offered large sums of money for the dog – he refused and man and dog went back to their regular work.

Two years later Bosun managed another extraordinary feat. He'd gone to the local railway station with Hale to collect some rearing equipment that was arriving by train. While Hale passed the time of day with the stationmaster and other staff, Bosun curled up on the platform and went to sleep. Some time later the train arrived and the rearing equipment was carried out to the waiting cart. It was then, as Hale got up behind the horses and prepared to set off for home, that he noticed Bosun was missing. He searched frantically around the station, the goods yard and around the fields beyond but there was no sign of the dog. This was extremely unusual, as Bosun had never been known to wander off before. As dusk fell Hale was forced to set off for home without the dog that had been his closest companion since he'd taken her home as a pup.

For several days there was no news at all in the district about the dog's fate but then an anonymous letter was pushed through the keeper's door. The writer claimed to have seen Bosun being dragged on to the train while Hale had been helping with the unloading. There was no way to verify this but Hale knew that the next station along the line was more than twenty miles away. On his next free day he caught the train, got off

at the next stop and asked local shopkeepers and station staff if they'd seen Bosun. No one had set eyes on the missing dog and Hale was forced to return home once again alone.

It is easy to imagine his astonishment when, two days later, he received a message from the stationmaster telling him that Bosun had just jumped off the down train and was waiting sitting happily by the stationmaster's fire waiting for his master.

No one ever discovered if Bosun had simply escaped from his kidnappers and by sheer good luck hopped on a train going in the right direction to take him home. But whatever the answer this escapade added hugely to the dog's reputation in the locality.

Bosun's last great adventure came many years later near the end of his life. He'd never lost his enthusiasm for shooting and would always work until he was exhausted – so much so that Hale, who was not normally sentimental about animals, began to think the dog should be given less arduous work. He would never admit it but the old keeper was worried that Bosun might die on him. But Bosun would have none of it and when Hale left him at home on shoot days the dog looked so miserable that the keeper quickly gave in and started taking him out again.

Half way through Bosun's last season he was out with his master picking up as usual when a ferocious storm blew up and the final drive of the day had to be abandoned. The Guns made their way through an increasingly terrifying blizzard to a narrow lane where an estate cart was waiting for them. It was then that Hale noticed that the oldest of the Guns was missing. Hale set off back through the blizzard with Bosun at his heels to find the man.

Visibility was poor by now as the light began to fail and the snowstorm grew increasingly violent. Hale checked along the line of the last drive but failed to see the old man. With no idea what else to try he tried to encourage Bosun out ahead of him to look. The dog seemed to grasp what was wanted almost immediately and set off on a line away from the ride where the last drive had taken place and into the wood.

Within minutes and despite the terrible storm he had found the old man. He had failed to see the others leaving and was quickly lost when the snow began to fall. He'd taken shelter under the trees and having no idea which direction might lead him to safety he had begun seriously to consider the possibility that he might die. When Hale told him that Bosun had found him virtually unaided the old man could hardly believe his ears. Just a few months later Bosun died in his sleep, probably from a heart attack.

10 Poachers' Tales

Cone catching

A century and more ago Guildford in Surrey was still a remote spot. Today it is part of the London commuter belt but in the mid 1800s it was a byword for poverty and backwardness and on the remote sandy commons round about locals gathered firewood, shot and snared rabbits and grazed their animals.

One day the local poacher decided he'd had enough of shooting rabbits so he decided he'd try for a pheasant on the edge of the local landowner's ground. He and a friend set off and had quickly bagged a couple of birds when the noise of their shooting brought out the keeper and they had to make a run for it.

Tempted once again by the lure of pheasants the old poacher and his young friend decided to try the same estate a week later. The young man called in at the poacher's isolated little cottage on the appointed day. While their morning tea was brewing the poacher took a few pages from a newspaper and cut them into eight-inch squares. He then twisted the squares into little cone-shaped packets and fitted them together one inside the other and popped them inside a sack.

'What on earth are they for?' asked the young man.

'You bide and see,' said the old poacher, who next gathered together a bag of grains of barley. Finally, he gathered together two more items – a thick, sharp-pointed iron poker about two feet long and a small bottle with a wooden screw top and a brush going down through the top into whatever liquid lay within.

The bottle, the young man discovered later, contained birdlime – a sort of sticky glue. The two men then set off across the fields, the poacher with his bag of bits and pieces, the young man, still hopeful of a shot or two, with his gun in hand. They walked about three miles until they came to a little used road. They went along this for some distance until they came to a gate. Here the poacher stopped and told the young man to wait and keep an eye out in case anyone should come along the road.

On the other side of the gate was a field about two hundred yards across and on its far side there was a wood. The poacher set off across the field disturbing a few pheasants as he went. Some of these ran while others flew into the wood. When he was within twenty yards of the trees he stopped and pulled out his iron poker. He pushed it into the ground and worked it in to make a hole a good bit bigger in diameter than the poker itself. Having made his hole he took out one of the paper cones and popped it into the hole. He then tipped in a few grains of barley and finally painted the edge of the inside of the cup with his birdlime brush. He then moved three or four yards away and repeated the whole operation. Continuing in this way, but keeping always parallel with the edge of the wood he made and filled about nine holes.

Pheasants will always run away from a stranger, but if they see him lingering near their home wood, especially if he stoops much of the time, they will keep their eyes fixed on him and the minute he goes they will come out to investigate what he's been up to. Before old Joe the poacher had got back to the gate where his young friend waited more than a dozen pheasants had come out to see what was going on.

A cock pheasant ran quickly across the grass and dipped its head into one of the holes to get at the barley. A second later, when it withdrew its head it was covered with the paper bag which the birdlime had stuck fast. The pheasant began to shake its head vigorously, but the paper bag stayed firmly in place. He then tried scratching at his head with his foot. Still no good. In the space of a minute three more birds were hopping around with paper bags on their heads. The young man offered to go and get them in case their strange appearance and behaviour might act as a warning to others, but the poacher knew better and the two simply stayed and waited. Within ten minutes nine pheasants were bagged. It was at this point that the old poacher pulled out a thin canvas bag and walked quickly out to where the birds were staggering around. Within seconds they had allowed themselves to be picked up as quietly as possible. When they returned to the keeper's cottage he told the young man that they could get a better price for the birds if they sold them to a man who would keep them for his aviary.

And that was the end of a successful day's poaching when not a shot was fired.

Ladies in waiting

Though the penalties for poaching were still harsh, many country people in the nineteenth century relied on pilfering game regularly simply to survive. Some poachers became legendary and many earned a reputation for untouchability. The police might know they were up to something but could never catch them red-handed.

Famous women poachers were a much rarer commodity, but two who stole game from a number of woodland areas around Oxford in the 1850s and 1860s became very well known indeed after they were caught and fined for their activities.

They escaped detection for a remarkably long time because no one expected women to be involved in poaching. For season after season no one took much notice of the two dishevelled and unkempt old women who always seemed to be smoking their pipes and loitering in the lanes when a pheasant shoot was in progress. Indeed it is doubtful if anyone realised till long afterwards that the two old women were always the same two old women regardless of whether the shoot was at Blenheim or at a remote farm. They seemed harmless enough, dottily jabbering to each other in an incomprehensible language everyone simply assumed was Romany.

They often wandered across to the Guns offering to sell them clothes pegs or little sprigs of rosemary or they were obsequiously helpful when it came to helping with the game cart.

It was only when an observant keeper kept an eye on them one day that he realised what was going on. When a drive began one or other of the two old women would wander along behind the Guns talking to their loaders or to anyone else who happened to be around. The other old woman waited in the lane and then, when the shooting had begun and no one was taking any notice of anything else, she upped and disappeared. When the keeper followed her he discovered that she was dodging into the edge of the wood through which the beaters were working their way towards the Guns. Once concealed in the edge of the wood she lifted her skirts and pulled a very small terrier out of a special bag sewn into her petticoats. Clearly highly trained and like all poachers' dogs taught above all to be absolutely quiet, the terrier immediately began rooting about in the thick undercover. Inevitably pheasants moving ahead of the beaters had already begun to concentrate here and it was easy for the terrier to catch half a dozen of these birds in less than ten minutes. If the terrier missed a bird and it clattered off into the sky, suspicion would not be aroused because it would just look as if the birds were starting to fly because the beaters were getting close to them.

When the terrier had caught a bird he carried it to the old woman who immediately wrung its neck and hung it by a special loop sewn into her underskirts. When she'd secured half a dozen birds the dog would get back into its special pouch and the old woman would wander back into the road and meet up with her friend. They might then hang around until the drive was over before congratulating the Guns and setting off for home.

The keeper who'd seen the two women at several shooting days earlier in the season was amazed at their audacity and the skill with which they

caught and hid the birds they'd poached. It was only because he knew what had gone on that the keeper noticed how much bigger one of the two women seemed at the end of the day than at the beginning.

When they were arrested they denied everything and became extremely abusive.

'I'd never in my life heard such foul language,' said the arresting policeman when he later gave evidence in court. 'One of them tried to hit me with one of the pheasants and even a Frenchman might have been horrified at the words they used – pure Billingsgate. We discovered they had a long list of convictions – everything from petty theft to impersonating women of quality.' The two were fined three shillings each.

Stovepipe heat

Victorian poachers were famously inventive and among a remarkable band of men few were more resourceful than John Connell who was said to be able to charm the birds out of the trees – even if the trees were just a few hundred feet from the keeper's cottage!

Connell tried various techniques for catching the keeper's birds silently – he tried poison, snaring and trapping but none seemed to work as well as he'd hoped.

After numerous experiments, brimstone burned at night under a tree in which birds were roosting became his favourite method. But how was the burning brimstone to be brought to the birds? Connell quickly came up with an answer. He persuaded the local blacksmith to make him a three-foot high stove that could be collapsed like a telescope. It was cylindrical and tapered at the top. The six tubes from which it was made fitted into each other perfectly. The stove had a few holes at the top to let the fumes out and vents to allow a draught of air in at the base. Fitted with a brimstone candle at the bottom the whole thing could be carried inconspicuously under a big top hat or in the folds of a large overcoat.

The blacksmith also made Connell two lightweight metal poles that fitted into recesses either side of the body of the stove. These would be used to carry the stove from tree to tree after the metal had become too hot to carry.

The poaching stove was far more successful even than Connell had hoped. On his first night time sortie, it took Connell just a few minutes under each tree to knock out dozens of pheasants – in total darkness he worked by listening for the soft thud as pheasants simply dropped like conkers.

Bane of the keepers

Poachers in Victorian times trained their dogs to work absolutely silently and really good poachers' dogs were often sold for large amounts of money such was the difficulty of training them never to bark.

Latimer Lee, a Lincolnshire poacher who died in 1905, was famous (or infamous) throughout rural Lincolnshire for his exploits. In a lifetime of poaching he had taken countless thousands of pheasants from local estates and was the bane of every keeper for miles around. He was also an expert at training silent dogs and none was cleverer or quieter than his own dog.

When Latimer was out looking for birds his dog would creep along well ahead of him searching for the first signs of danger either in the form of the police or a keeper. If the dog sensed anyone was there it would race back to Latimer and put its head in his hand. That was the danger signal and it meant Latimer knew well in advance that trouble was brewing and it was time to go home.

In all matters except poaching Latimer was regarded as scrupulously honest. He often claimed that he saw poaching as a poor man's revenge on the rich and that therefore it was a perfectly reasonable thing to do. In every sphere of life other than taking hares, pheasants and other game birds he never dreamt of cheating and it was his reputation for honest dealing that got him off the hook during one of his rare court appearances.

He'd been out poaching and had successfully caught half a dozen pheasants, which were safely hung up in his shed. With the week's birds safely gathered he decided to go shopping and stopped at a farm to collect a large bag of onions. Carrying on towards the nearest town he met a policeman who promptly arrested him!

By eleven o'clock the next morning Latimer was in the dock and facing the magistrate. The policeman who had arrested Latimer was new to the district but knowing the poacher's reputation he simply assumed that pretty much everything the man did was probably illegal.

The policeman's case was based entirely on Latimer's bag of onions, which he was accused of having stolen. Latimer was genuinely outraged.

'Stealing onions!' he gasped. 'Stealing onions! Why, I'd scorn to do such a thing. You all know what my business is. I'm a poacher. I wouldn't lower myself to onions!'

The case was dismissed. The magistrate knew that, old rogue though he was, Latimer would never belittle himself by stealing vegetables.

Rats!

A Surrey poacher who worked in the woods and fields near Mitcham in Surrey towards the end of the nineteenth century was so well known to the police that they stopped him regularly just on the off-chance that they might find incriminating evidence on him.

So they were delighted one morning when they came across him carrying a large sack up the high street as if he didn't care who saw him. The police pounced, convinced they'd caught him red handed. He protested his innocence saying there was nothing in the bag that could possibly interest the police. But there was something alive in the sack, the poacher had a reputation and the police were keen to nail their man. Poacher and police set off for the local police station where, after much discussion and argument, the contents of the bag were tipped out on to the floor.

Immediately the scene was one of pandemonium as nearly thirty huge rats immediately dashed for cover in every direction. The police evacuated the police station, which had to be shut down for the rest of the day.

The poacher roared with laughter and refused to help the police.

Instead he wandered off to the pub leaving the constabulary scratching their heads.Eventually the police offered to go easy on him in future and the poacher agreed to go in and catch the rats.

Irish wit

Poaching is almost a fact of life in the countryside, although the modern poacher has given poaching a very bad name because he often kills on a large scale and does it indiscriminately. The old-style poacher took a few birds for the pot and to supplement what was usually a poverty-line existence and he did it at great personal risk.

Until the early nineteenth century a man could be hanged for taking a pheasant and the rights of property were such that keepers were perfectly entitled to shoot a poacher on sight, but keepers often tolerated poachers provided they didn't over-step the mark and take too many birds. Some even allowed a poacher to take a few birds each week if he promised to keep all the other poachers away!

Many poachers became famous for their exploits and for their ready wit, which was most often displayed in the courtroom. A famous Irish poacher was known for his wit – and his speed. He was a champion runner and if challenged he simply bolted and it was only on the rarest occasions, usually when he was surrounded, that he was apprehended. He was also an excellent shot and on more than one occasion he cheekily offered to give the local gentry shooting lessons.

Eventually his luck ran out and he was caught and charged. He'd managed to dispose of his birds so there was little hard evidence against him, but he was taken before the local magistrate.

The magistrate then called a witness for the prosecution who was actually a friend of the poacher. He was also a man whose brilliance and slipperiness in argument was legendary.

After the accusation that the poacher had fired at a certain place on a certain day the magistrate asked the witness: 'Did you see the defendant shoot?'

'No, I only heard him,' came the reply.

'Then your evidence is not satisfactory. You may stand down,' said the magistrate.

The witness turned his back on the judge and started to walk down the steps out of the witness box laughing loudly. Outraged by this total lack of respect for the court the magistrate made the witness return to the stand.

'How dare you laugh in court' said the magistrate. 'Do you realise it is tantamount to contempt of court, a serious offence?'

'Did you see me laugh your honour?' asked the witness.

'No sir, but I heard you,' was the angry reply.

'Then your evidence is not satisfactory, you may stand down,' said the witness with a grin.

The packed court dissolved in howls of laughter.

Another poaching tale from Ireland emphasises the country people's dislike of anything to do with the law or, more particularly, lawyers. The hatred of lawyers meant the local people were always delighted when someone got one over on a barrister or solicitor. It didn't happen often but when it did it was remembered for many years and the tale would be told and retold throughout the district much to the chagrin of the lawyer in question.

An immensely fat, English, red-faced lawyer who appeared regularly in cases involving the prosecution of locals for petty offences, was heartily disliked. He would talk to the country people as if they were fools and they resented this hugely, but could do little about it.

On a day that became legendary the lawyer, who weighed at least twenty stone, was in court prosecuting a poacher who had been caught with a few rabbits in a bag. The man was poor and had a large family so there was much support for him.

The defendant called an old blind woman from his village to give evidence in his defence. He said that he'd called out to her from his garden that evening and that, as he'd spent the whole evening in his garden working and had spoken to her every now and then, he could not have been out looking for other people's game in the woods round about.

The lawyer said to the judge: 'My Lord, we cannot admit this woman's evidence as she cannot have seen a thing. She did not see the accused in his garden and he may have slipped away to the woods between his occasional remarks to her. And voices over a distance may be mistook.'

On hearing this, the old woman turned her head toward where she knew the judge would be sitting and said: 'I'm blind and have been since birth, but I never mistake a man's voice. It's like feeling a man's face – it'll always tell me who he is as good as if I could see him plain in front of me.'

'My Lord' repeated the lawyer, 'I merely repeat what I have already said.'

The judge said: 'I think it we can hear the witness's evidence. I am sure the blind are indeed able to identify people by the feel of their faces.'

The lawyer thought he would prove his point by putting his face close to the old woman's and then disguising his voice: 'Now my dear,' said the lawyer in a guttural tone, 'who have we here?'

The old woman said: 'I do not recognise that voice, but put your face up to me and I will put my hand on it and know you in a second.'

The lawyer leant forward until his face was within a few inches of the old woman's and she put her hand out and touched him. She then turned towards the judge and said: 'It's a terrible thing, your honour, to make fun of a poor old blind woman. This is no face at all I'm feeling. Sure it's a great soft, fat arse!'

There was so much laughter that the case had to be adjourned while order was restored and the poacher had so far gained the sympathy of the court by the time the proceedings resumed that the case against him was dismissed.

Get your skates on!

The Fenland region of England – that vast area running from the Wash in Lincolnshire down through Norfolk and Cambridgeshire – was once a remote and inaccessible region of marsh and reed bed, swamp and quagmire until Dutch engineers drained the water and created a profitable if bleak region of empty farmland.

The men of the fens who lived and worked in that rich watery world were by any standards remarkable characters. To make ends meet they worked at any number of seasonal jobs – from shooting wildfowl in winter to catching eels in summer and with a bit of farm labouring here and there. Until the 1930s and the advent of purpose-built rinks, Britain's greatest ice skaters also came from the Fens.

Skating had come to the area with the Dutch engineers who began draining the peaty waters in the seventeenth century and by the end of the nineteenth century the local men and women were masters of the art. Until well into the twentieth century they still used iron blades lashed with leather thongs to the soles of an old pair of boots. In earlier times they'd used animal bones!

East Anglia was ideal for skating because the land flooded every year and as the floods were often shallow and widespread they turned quickly to ice.

The skates and the frozen fields no doubt gave the locals a huge amount of pleasure, but they also gave the local poachers huge advantages over the local constabulary. The poachers would strap on their boots, sling a gun and a game bag over their shoulders and skate quietly along any frozen stretch of water that brought them within range of a wood. Within minutes of shooting a bird they would be half a mile away, hurtling skilfully over the ice before the local keeper had any idea anything was amiss.

But at least one poacher came unstuck when a crafty policeman got wind of what was going on in his area and lay in wait at the edge of a frozen field where dozens of pheasants had already been spirited away. When dawn came the policeman spotted a figure with a gun speeding silently across the ice. The figure stopped at the edge of the wood and waited. A few moments later he fired into the trees at the roosting pheasants. With a brace in his bag he was about to set off for home when he heard the policeman's shout. Not in the least worried, the poacher pushed off and built up a bit of speed on the ice, chuckling to himself as he went. Imagine his horror when he glanced back only to see the policeman belting after him and also on skates. The poacher was apprehended and fined three shillings.

Feminine wiles

There was a famous Victorian rabbit poacher who evaded the local keepers for many years. They could never understand how the man was able to vanish so completely each time there was a report that a poacher had been seen on the land. Then someone noticed that whenever the mystery poacher was around and the keepers hurried to the place where he'd been sighted a village woman always seemed to be around. It was only much later that everyone realised the woman was in fact the poacher.

Buck, as she was known, eventually became so famous – precisely because women poachers were rare - that she couldn't poach at all. She was a gamekeeper's daughter and knew the woods inside out. She'd started to poach after marrying a man addicted to drink who was never in work and she was said to know more about snaring and trapping than any man alive. She knew also how to sneak into a pheasant wood at night and shoot the birds roosting – and she could shoot them almost silently. One extraordinary night she bagged over thirty pheasants with her gun and not a sound was heard. She later revealed her secret. Her old muzzleloader had been adapted to break down into short pieces that could be hidden in her skirts and she loaded it with tiny amounts of black powder. On the night in question she used all her lifetime's poaching skills to get within a few yards of each bird before firing each tiny charge. She'd chosen a windy night too so the little puff of sound would be hidden and her clothes were specially adapted with numerous hooks and bags and secret pockets. In these she stowed her birds and shuffled home as happy as the cat that got the cream.